MALAYSIA

MALAYSIA

Recipes from a family kitchen

PING COOMBES

To my mum who taught me what good food is, to Alexa my daughter who inspires me to be a better cook every day, and to my husband Andrew who supports and loves me unconditionally.

Food has the power to create and evoke memories.

CONTENTS

INTRODUCTION

Hello, I'm Ping! In addition to being wife to my long-suffering husband Andrew and mother to my beautiful, cheeky daughter Alexa, my obsession in life is spreading the love for Malaysian food and flavours. I'm so passionate about Malaysian food, I entered MasterChef 2014 so that I could get the word out about this wonderful cuisine from my home country. And I won! This book is so precious to me as each dish is created with memories from my childhood and interwoven are pieces of my family's history, my travels and my love of food. I want to show you just how easy, joyful and delicious Malaysian food can be.

MY MALAYSIA

I grew up in Malaysia, in a city called Ipoh – famous for its limestone caves, pomelo, bean sprouts and women. Women, I hear you say? Yes – legend has it that the limestone mountains around Ipoh protect the purity of the air and water; therefore Ipoh women are more beautiful than anywhere else in Malaysia.

My mum did most of the cooking at home, and when she was working, my grandmother (popo) would take over. My grandmother migrated to Malaysia from China when my dad was just a few days old, and she brought with her the influences of Hakka cooking – a cuisine from northern China that often features preserved pork and vegetables.

When I wasn't tearing around the neighbourhood on my bicycle, or fighting with my brother, I would stand in the kitchen to watch Mum cook. There was always a wok, a soup pot and a rice cooker on the go. My mum would rise early in the morning, visit the local wet market, come home, put a soup over a low heat on the charcoal hob outside, then go to work. We would wake up to the sweet smell of soy-braised pork belly and fragrant chicken broth wafting through the house. It would simmer gently all day so that when she came home from work, all she would have to do is add the finishing touches.

Watching my mum cook was mesmerising: she knew exactly what to put in – there were no scales or measuring spoons in sight – and she was always so quick.

Every evening, my mum would call out for us: 'Ping, Boy,' (my brother's nickname) 'sek fan la!' (meaning 'come eat your dinner'). The first thing we'd be met with would be the intoxicating smell, followed by the sight of a sumptuous feast of at least three different dishes and a broth.

Occasionally my mum would attempt what she called 'English' food, which included a kind of Asian spaghetti bolognese, her infamous chicken pies, and stews with potatoes and star anise. Despite her dubious interpretations of western food I loved all these dishes, and it felt like such a novelty to be eating something different to our usual staples. In light of this, I've included a chapter on 'English' food to pay tribute to my mum's delicious experimental recipes.

It was only in my early twenties, when I came to the UK to go to university, that I started to cook for myself.

I go back to Malaysia every year to visit family and friends, and every trip revolves around food. Throughout the year, Andrew and I make a list of what we want to eat on our upcoming trip, and tick them off as we go along: our list might consist of satay – sweet and smoky slivers of meat grilled to order and served with spicy peanut sauce; nasi lemak – coconut rice with sambal ikan bilis, my winning main course on MasterChef; and soft chicken 'hor fun' noodles in Ipoh Old Town where I ate as a child and recently took Alexa. These for me are the tastes and aromas of home, which I hope I've captured in this book.

MALAYSIA ON A PLATE

So, what is Malaysian food? Good question! I was once asked in an interview why Malaysian food is relatively unknown in the UK compared to Thai or Japanese. I gave it some thought and realised the answer isn't straightforward. To understand Malaysian food is to understand how Malaysia is made up. The country consists largely of three races: Malays, Chinese and Indians. Imagine the array of flavours and influences just from these three cultures. It's difficult to pinpoint one distinct dish or flavour and call it 'Malaysian', as Malaysian cuisine is a fusion of all these cultures.

Peranakan or Nyonya cuisine combines Chinese ingredients with a Malay cooking method. Peranakans are descendants of early Chinese migrants who settled in Penang and Malacca. The flavours in this cuisine are spicy, tangy and aromatic and use a lot of chillies, lemongrass, Kaffir lime, dried shrimps, shrimp paste and tamarind. Nyonya dishes in this book include Ayam Kapitan (page 151), a spicy, moreish, aromatic chicken curry with a slight tang, and my mum's secret recipe for Sambal Prawns (page 177) – prawns cooked in a tangy lemongrass and chilli sauce.

Then there is the Malaysian Mamak fare. Mamak is the name for the Indian Muslim community in Malaysia. Mamak street-food stalls look pretty basic with stainless steel tables and they stay open until late at night – some are even open 24 hours a day. They serve up dishes like Roti Canai (page 68) – a delicious flaky bread cooked on the griddle, which is great with curry; Teh Tarik (page 232) – translated as 'pulled tea', where the vendor pours strong, sweet tea from one jug to another; and Mee Goreng Mamak (page 121) – fried noodles with a spicy, sweet and sticky sauce.

Malaysian food to me is just so exciting, with its almost never-ending variation of flavours, textures and smells. I want to show you how easy it is to recreate the flavours I grew up with, using ingredients easily sourced in your local supermarkets. I also tell you how to store and use ingredients in different ways so that nothing goes to waste, and most of the recipes do not require much preparation or a long, daunting list of ingredients. A few require a little effort, but I promise you it's worthwhile.

I hope this book will entice you to discover this hidden gem of a cuisine. Most importantly, I want you to have fun making the dishes and to put a smile on the faces of the people you cook for. Every recipe has its own story and in each there is an expression of sharing love through food. I'd like to share all of this with you.

Happy cooking and happy eating

MY PANTRY

Not long ago, a friend took one look at my little pantry and said, 'It looks like an Oriental supermarket in there!'. She was completely fascinated by the rows of ingredients in their glass jars, ranging from shiitake mushrooms and dried shrimps to dried chillies.

To create Malaysian dishes at home, I always have these ingredients to hand, either in the fridge, the freezer or the pantry. Here I have included ways of storing them where applicable, so that you can stretch them that much further and avoid wastage. You can find all of these ingredients in your local supermarket or Oriental supermarket.

HERBS, LEAVES, STEMS AND BUDS

1. CORIANDER
A fragrant herb used a lot in South-east Asian cooking. It is particularly great with curries, stir-fries and fritters. Leftover coriander can be frozen.

2. CURRY LEAVES
This potent herb is commonly used to flavour curries. It is often found dry in the herb section of the supermarket, but I always use fresh leaves, which you can find in a lot of Indian shops. Buy a big bunch, remove the leaves and place them in a freezer bag. Freeze, and when you're ready to use them, just drop them into curries straight from the freezer.

3. KAFFIR LIME LEAVES
These are the citrus leaves of Kaffir limes. They are usually sold dried or frozen. I recommend buying the frozen/fresh leaves and keeping them in the freezer. They defrost quickly and have a better flavour than the dried ones. They are often crushed to add to curries, or thinly sliced to add to a salad. I add them to drinks, too (page 237).

4. LEMONGRASS
My favourite herb of all time. As the name suggests, it is a type of grass, and in Malaysia you can find it growing at the back of houses or by the

roadside. I use it in practically everything I cook, savoury and sweet. Only use the tender bottom half of the lemongrass. I cut away 10–15cm of the stem, then peel off the first layer to reveal the tender core, which is less fibrous. Lemongrass freezes well: freezing it seems to break down its fibres and make it more pliable and easy to chop. I like to use the leftover tops in drinks (page 237).

5. PANDAN LEAVES

Also known as screw pine leaves and regarded as 'the vanilla of the east', pandan leaves have a subtle, sweet and fragrant smell. They are often used to add flavour to rice or Malaysian desserts. The intense colour of the leaves can also be used as a natural food pigment. The leaves can be frozen and keep well in the fridge for a couple of weeks. To use them as a flavouring, scrunch them up to release their fragrance then knot them and nestle them in the pan. To use them as a natural colouring, cut the leaves into small pieces, blend with water, then drain the water through a fine-mesh sieve into a bowl to extract the green juice (discard the leaf fibres).

6. THAI BASIL

This is another fragrant herb that has a citrusy note. Great with stir-fries, stews and dips. It is normally sold fresh, with stalks intact, in Oriental supermarkets. It can be frozen and still maintain its flavour.

7. TORCH GINGER BUD

Known as 'bunga kantan', this has a citrusy smell and is used to flavour salads and curries. It's tricky to source fresh buds in the UK, however they can be found in the form of purées in Oriental supermarkets.
I have adapted the recipe on page 79 to suit the puréed version, so that the flavour of this lovely bud comes through without having to use the fresh stuff.

CHILLIES AND SPICES

There are hundreds if not thousands of varieties of chillies. There are
a couple of chilli farms near my home so when the farmer allows me,
I go and pick them myself while quizzing him on how spicy they are.
The majority of the time, I buy chillies from my local supermarket. The
most commonly cultivated chillies, and those red and green ones you
usually find in the supermarket, are of the C. annuum species. They are
4–7cm long and are usually found in mixed packets of green and red.
The red ones are a bit of pot luck in terms of heat! Before using them,
cut one open and dab your finger in it then taste, to test the level of
spiciness. If it blows your head off, use it sparingly.

 Most of the spices in this book, such as ground cumin, star anise,
ground coriander and five-spice, will probably be lurking at the back
of your store cupboard. However, I've listed some others here that you

might be less familiar with, but which I regularly use. I recommend buying spices at Oriental supermarkets as they are cheaper than other shops and the turnover of spices is faster, so they are often fresher.

8. BIRD'S EYE CHILLIES
These are tiny little chillies that really pack a punch. You can find them in small packs in supermarkets and quite often you will only need one or two. They freeze well and as they defrost quickly they can be taken out just when you need them.

9. CANDLENUT
This nut resembles a large chickpea. You can't eat them raw but added to curry pastes they act as a thickening agent. If you can't find them, substitute them with macadamia nuts. The nuts are best stored in glass jars somewhere dark and dry.

10. DRIED CHILLIES
Dried chillies are sometimes used instead of fresh ones, to add heat, pungency and colour to a dish – I like to use Kashmiri chillies. I sometimes combine dried and fresh ones to make curry pastes (pages 32–33), which you can store in sterilised, sealed jars.

11. GALANGAL
This is a type of rhizome very similar to ginger. It has a citrusy smell and is great in curries and soy-based stews. Galangal is more fibrous than ginger, so do be cautious when handling it with a knife. Like ginger, you can scrape the outer skin away with the edge of a spoon.

12. GINGER
Ginger is a very versatile ingredient. It imparts a fragrant yet warming flavour. It's found in savoury and sweet dishes in Malaysia, and is called 'halia'. Ginger is commonly used in Malaysia in spice pastes, dips, stir-fries and marinades.

13. MALAYSIAN CURRY POWDER
This is a blend of spices suitable for Malaysian curry dishes. If you can't find it, you can use Madras curry powder.

14. STAR ANISE
This look like a petal and smells like aniseed. Used in moderation, it is a great spice to flavour curries, stews and desserts.

FLAVOURINGS AND SEASONINGS

In addition to fresh ingredients, herbs and spices, flavourings and seasonings help elevate natural flavours to new heights.

15. CHICKEN STOCK POWDER
I use this instead of stock cubes. I use the Knorr powder, which you can buy in tubs. I recommend powder over cubes, as you can use the exact amount you need, without returning half-used cubes to languish in your cupboard.

16. CHILLI SAUCE
Maggi Sos Cili is the best chilli sauce out there, in my humble opinion. It is slightly sweet but has just enough heat to give its rival – sweet chilli sauce – a run for its money. It is delicious served with fried chicken skins (page 58) and pretty much anything else!

17. SWEET SOY SAUCE
Known as kecap manis, this is a little thicker and sweeter than light soy sauce. I often use it to balance out the saltiness of light soy sauce. The two brands I like are Lee Kum Kee and Kipas, and you can find both in Oriental supermarkets.

18. LIGHT SOY SAUCE
I use light soy sauce throughout this book, unless otherwise stated. Made from fermented soya beans, salt, water and wheat flour, it is a very common flavouring and is widely available. My favourite brand is Pearl River. Tamari is a great gluten-free soy sauce alternative.

19. OYSTER SAUCE
This is a thick, rich sauce made with extracts of oyster. It is very versatile and works well alongside light soy sauce to flavour food. Lee Kum Kee oyster sauce is my brand of choice.

20. PLUM SAUCE
I like to use a clear plum sauce which is quite runny, unlike the thick, syrupy ones. It is light in flavour and not overly sweet, and it makes a lovely dipping sauce and a good base for sweet and sour chicken. My favourite brand is Healthy Boy.

21. RICE WINE VINEGAR

This is vinegar made out of rice, which carries a sweetness. It is quite expensive compared to white wine vinegar or distilled vinegar, which you can substitute it with if you don't have rice wine vinegar.

22. SRIRACHA

This is a Thai hot sauce made from chilli peppers, vinegar, garlic, sugar and salt. It can be quite acidic but makes a lovely dipping sauce. Use another acidic chilli sauce flavoured with garlic if you can't find sriracha.

23. SWEET CHILLI SAUCE

This is the most widely known of all chilli sauces, and it is sweeter than the others. It makes a great dipping sauce.

STORE CUPBOARD ESSENTIALS

24. CHINESE SAUSAGE

These sausages are preserved and perfumed with rice wine. They add great flavour to dishes like my Clay Pot Chicken Rice (page 102). Choose the plain pork ones (not the ones with liver) and use them much like you would use bacon.

25. BLACK BEANS

Made from soya beans, these have been fermented in salt and must be rinsed in water before using. They are delicious cooked in chilli and garlic dishes.

26. COCONUT MILK

Rich and silky, this is used in a lot of Malaysian curries and desserts, giving them a sweet and fragrant aroma. It comes in cans and is widely available. If you have leftover coconut milk, pour it into ice cube trays and freeze, then you can add it to curries straight from frozen.

27. CORNFLOUR

This flour is ground from dried maize and is a useful ingredient for binding and tenderising meat. It is also a good gluten-free flour to use if you want to thicken a sauce. Beware of using too much in sauces, however, as this will result in a slimy texture.

30

36

41

29

24

35

39

25

31

28

28. DRIED ANCHOVIES

These are essential for making Sambal Ikan Bilis for Nasi Lemak (page 107), and are a good source of protein when added to broths (pages 83–85 and 91). Near my home town of Ipoh there is a fishing village called Lumut, where I was shown how dried anchovies are produced. The fishermen boil the freshly caught anchovies on board, with salt water to preserve them. When they come back to the harbour, they dry them in the sun. They are usually sold whole in packets in the UK, but in Malaysia you can pay a little extra to have them skinned and gutted. Store in glass jars in a cool, dry place.

29. DRIED SHIITAKE MUSHROOMS

Also known as Chinese mushrooms, you can find these in Oriental supermarkets. The dried mushrooms keep indefinitely in a cool, dry place. To use, rehydrate them by soaking them in water for about two hours, then discard the stalks. For plumper mushrooms with a better texture, marinate in a little oil and sugar for 1 hour before using.

30. DRIED SHRIMPS

These are tiny shrimps that are boiled in salted water, drained and then dried in the sun. They add umami to a dish and keep well, either in the fridge or in a cool, dry place.

31. DRIED WOOD EAR MUSHROOMS

These are also called black fungus. They look like black orange peel and can be found near the dried shiitake mushrooms in Oriental supermarkets. To use, rehydrate them for one hour, then rinse them under cold water and discard any hard stubs. They do not have much flavour, but give a lovely texture to dishes such as spring rolls, dumplings, salads and stir-fries. My mum believes wood ear mushrooms help with blood circulation and are especially valuable for women who have just given birth.

32. GUNPOWDER TEA

Originating in China, this tea takes its name from the tea leaves that resemble black gunpowder. It is this that forms the base for my Pandan Tea (page 232) and Iced Lemongrass Tea (page 235). The dry tea leaves keep well for a long time in a cool, dry place.

33. OILS

All the oil used in this book is vegetable oil, unless otherwise stated. You can use sunflower instead or other flavourless oils. Don't use any flavoured oil such as olive or sesame oil unless stated.

34. PALM SUGAR

This rich, dark brown sweetener is tapped from palm trees. The sugar is extracted by boiling the sap until thick and then strained into bamboo tubes to harden. Palm sugar has a very rich flavour without being overly-sweet, and it is used in a lot of Malaysian desserts, such as my Malaysian Coconut-filled Pancakes (page 222).

35. PICKLED LETTUCE

These crunchy pickles come in jars or cans and can be found in most Oriental supermarkets. Pickled in soy sauce and sugar, they are a lovely mix of salty and sweet, and make a great accompaniment to Congee (page 108).

36. SALTED EGGS

These are duck eggs preserved in brine, which require cooking before eating. To cook salted eggs, boil them for 15 minutes then – as soon as they are cool enough to handle – cut them in half lengthways and scrape the insides out. Discard the shell. I particularly love them with Congee (page 108) and I also use them as a coating for my Crispy Squid in Salted Egg Yolks (page 178) or simply eat them with white rice and sambals (I like to mash the egg whites and add them to fried rice). Keep them in an airtight container in the fridge once shelled and abide by the use-by date. The container should have a lovely salty eggy smell when you open it, but if it smells strong and you get a whiff of ammonia, do not use.

37. CENTURY EGGS

These may look strange with the whites turned brown and the yolks dark green, but they're seriously delicious. I love to eat mine with pickled ginger or alongside Congee (page 108).

38. SHRIMP PASTE

There are two types of shrimp paste: dried (usually sold in blocks – the best ones are made in Penang) and a softer type sold in tubs. To bring out the full flavour of the dried paste, it would traditionally be toasted on an open fire, but you can achieve the same result by toasting dried paste in a frying pan over a low heat until fragrant. To store, when cooled, wrap in baking parchment then foil and chill. It will keep indefinitely. The softer variety of paste requires no toasting. The flavour is less pungent, but it's easier to store and use, and keeps for a long time in the fridge.

39. SPRING ROLL SKINS
These are sold in a variety of sizes and always come frozen. One of my favourite brands is TJs, which can be found in Oriental supermarkets. They are great deep-fried but can also be eaten fresh.

40. TAPIOCA FLOUR
This is made from the cassava plant and is another good gluten-free alternative. Like cornflour, it is used to bind meats and works especially well when deep-frying as it adds a lovely crispness.

41. WONTON WRAPPERS
Sold frozen in packs usually found near the spring roll sheets in Oriental supermarkets, these come cut to size, ready for wrapping. There are two types: standard (which I use in this book) and those more suitable for deep-frying.

SOYA BEAN PRODUCTS

Soya beans are used to make products like tofu (bean curd) and soy sauce; both popular ingredients in Malaysian cooking. It is packed full of protein and rumour has it among the Chinese that it will give you a smooth complexion!

42. BEAN CURD PUFF
These dried and fried pieces of tofu with pockets of air inside can be found at Oriental supermarkets. Bean curd puff is wonderful in sauces and soups, as it absorbs the flavours around it. I used them in the Nyonya Curry Laksa (page 115).

43. BEAN CURD STICKS
This is the skin that forms on top of boiling milk, which is dried and twisted into sticks. These go wonderfully in stir-fries and soups.

44. FIRM TOFU

Dense and stronger in flavour than the silken type, this is the tofu most commonly found in supermarkets. It is great in stir-fries as it holds its shape, and it keeps in the fridge for up to five days after opening.

45. RED FERMENTED BEAN CURD

This come in cans or jars, usually in cube form. Ask someone to help you find it in the Oriental supermarket, as the labeling can be confusing. Fermented bean curd adds a big hit of umami and is strong in flavour, so should be used in moderation. I love using it in my Red Pork Belly Nuggets (page 143) and Red Braised Pork Ribs (page 144). Once opened, keep in the fridge in glass jars.

RICE AND NOODLES

46. BLACK GLUTINOUS RICE

This is an unmilled rice with a dark purple colour. It has a nutty flavour and chewy texture and in South-east Asia it's often used in desserts.

47. FLAT RICE NOODLES

These gluten-free noodles are sold dry in packets and can be found in most supermarkets. To rehydrate, soak them in boiling water for 30 minutes and drain. Coat with oil to avoid sticking. You can find fresh noodles in Oriental supermarkets, which are softer in texture than the dry ones. They are flat and are about 2cm wide.

48. MUNG BEAN NOODLES/GLASS NOODLES

These gluten-free noodles are made from mung beans (not to be confused with rice vermicelli, as they look very similar in their dry form). They are sold in Oriental supermarkets in convenient individual 50g packets. To rehydrate them, soak them in boiling water for 5 minutes and drain. They are great in salads and spring rolls, as they absorb any flavours you throw at them.

49. RICE VERMICELLI/RICE NOODLES

These gluten-free, thread-like noodles are available fresh and dried in larger supermarkets or Oriental supermarkets. The time it takes to rehydrate the dried noodles depends on the brand, but it usually takes just 5 minutes. They soak up broths and sauces well. You can also find them fresh in bags in the stir-fry section of supermarkets.

52

47

43

49

46

48

51

50. UDON NOODLES
Thick, round wheat noodles sold semi-fresh in compressed packets, you can find these in Oriental supermarkets. They are ready to use straight out of the packet and are a great staple to keep in the pantry.

51. WONTON NOODLES
These fresh noodles are sold in portioned packets that resemble balls of wool (one ball is enough for one person). They're versatile and freeze well. You can boil them from frozen and they will be ready to use in three minutes.

52. YELLOW EGG NOODLES
You can find these cooked and dried in your local supermarket. The cooked ones can be tipped from the packet, straight into your stir-fries. Dried noodles should be cooked according to the packet instructions.

SHORTCUT INGREDIENTS

53. CRISPY PRAWN CHILLIES AND CRISPY IKAN BILIS
If you like spicy foods, you'll love these. I eat them with practically everything, from rice and noodles to boiled eggs and vegetables. If you don't fancy making the Shrimp Chilli Oil (page 43) you can substitute that with this.

54. CRISPY SHALLOTS
Ready-made crispy shallots are a must-have in my pantry. Some things are just not worth making at home and this is one of them. Home-fried shallots tend to be more bitter than shop-bought ones, which are sweet, crunchy and go with just about everything. Italians have Parmesan, Asians have crispy shallots.

55. MALAYSIAN BEEF RENDANG PASTE
You can buy ready-made rendang paste it you don't tancy making it fresh (page 157). Disregard what it says on the packet about the rendang being ready in 30 minutes – a good rendang needs time and patience: two hours minimum cooking time. I always add additional herbs and spices such as cinnamon, lemongrass and Kaffir limes leaves, to make it more indulgent and fragrant.

56. MALAYSIAN CURRY PASTE

Though I include a recipe for this (page 32), you can buy it ready-made, to use in a variety of curries, such as my Malaysian Chicken Curry (page 148). It's always handy to have in the cupboard.

57. MALAYSIAN LAKSA PASTE

If you have the time, do try my recipe (page 33) but ready-made pastes are pretty good and I have packets of them in my pantry for those desperate times.

58. PRAWN NOODLE PASTE

To make this rich, spicy paste from scratch, you'd need lots and lots of prawn shells, which obviously aren't readily available. In the absence of those, this shop-bought version is handy and I use it in my Cheat's Prawn Noodles (page 127). Store in a cool, dry place, and once opened keep in the fridge.

59. TAMARIND CONCENTRATE

Tamarind is a fruit that gives acidity to a dish. It is commonly used in Asia instead of lime or lemon juice and is usually sold in a block of pulp and seeds. To extract the juice, warm water is added to the pulp, mashed and then strained. A friend of mine introduced me to ready-made tamarind concentrate, which is sold in jars or bottles so the mashing is unnecessary and the concentrate is ready to use. Once opened, keep in the fridge.

COOK'S NOTES

We eat very differently in Malaysia to how we eat in Europe. We don't divide our meal up into starters, mains and desserts. Rather, we share everything on the table, passing it around as we go, and eat as the dishes arrive (and without much constraint). I have written this book in sections which focus on the types of dishes in Malaysian cuisine. Some dishes are more suitable for snacks and some are substantial enough to be eaten on their own or accompanied by rice or noodles. Feel free to mix things up.

EQUIPMENT

I don't have crazy gadgets; I cook with normal pots and pans. But, there are a few items I use regularly that you might not have, but which would prove to be super-useful.

1. CLAY POT

Clay or earthenware pots come in all manner of different sizes. The one I use is medium sized, and has a glazed interior. They are cheap and can be found in large Oriental supermarkets. Clay pots retain heat really well, so they cook food more evenly and quicker, and keep it warmer for longer. You can put them directly onto the hob or in the oven, but they do not work on induction hobs.

Clay pots are very good for braising. They are also attractive vessels, so I often serve dishes straight out of the clay pot. Just be sure to put something heat resistant underneath the pot to avoid damaging your table. If you do not have a clay pot, you can use a small cast-iron casserole dish.

When using a clay pot for the first time, submerge it in cold water for one hour before using it. Then drain it and leave it to dry at room temperature for 24 hours. Do not put it in the dishwasher. Although clay pots can withstand high temperatures they cannot withstand a fast fluctuation in temperature or a sudden temperature change. So don't put a cold clay pot over a high heat: instead, bring it up to temperature gently. As it holds heat well, you only need to cook over a medium heat. If you haven't used your clay pot for a while, wash it well before use so that it doesn't get too dry (to reduce the risk of cracking).

2. METAL WOK

A wok is a very useful piece of equipment. They come in two forms: round-bottomed and flat-bottomed. Round-bottomed woks are designed to sit better on wok burners and the flat ones are better for using on gas or induction hobs. Here in the UK, people only use woks for stir-fries but you can use them for all kinds of cooking techniques: to steam (see Steamed Hake with Garlic Oil and Oyster Sauce on page 164); braise (see Beef Rendang on page 157, Captain's Chicken Curry on page 151, Red Braised Pork Ribs on page 144); pan-fry (see Pan-fried Seabass with Kecap Manis on page 167, Egg Foo Yung with Choi Sum and Onion on page 195); deep-fry (see Chilli Crab with Fried Manton on page 170, Turmeric 'Mamak Style' Fried Chicken on page 146); or use as a bain-marie (see Caramel Coconut Curd on page 215). In fact, most recipes in this book have been tested using a wok. I have three!

When using a wok for the first time, season it by stir-frying chopped spring onions, ginger and regular onions over a medium–high heat, until they are crisp and burnt. Move the vegetables around the wok continuously so they coat the interior of the wok. Discard the burnt vegetables and scrub the wok clean. Drain and heat up the wok on the hob for 10 seconds for any excess water to evaporate. Once dry, turn off the heat and rub the wok with a thin layer of vegetable oil. Every time you wash the wok, make sure you oil it to prevent it from rusting.

3. RUBBER SPATULA

This is very useful for stirring and for scraping the last bits of spice mix off your pan or wok, and for scraping out every ounce of paste from your blender.

PASTES, SAMBALS AND CONDIMENTS

So many of the tantalising flavours in Malaysian dishes stem from their essential foundation: the paste. Making a paste yourself is a labour of love and while you can buy them if you're short on time, the richness of the home-made versions are hard to beat. If you fancy having a go at making your own curry pastes, the recipes here form the basis of many of the dishes in this book.

If you haven't come across a sambal before, the best way to describe it is like a sauce-come-chutney. Sambals are very common in Malaysia and are usually spicy, and we use them to accompany a meal or to form parts of other dishes. This chapter features some of my favourite sambals. I use fresh red chillies alongside dried ones to create attractive and intense sambals – my mum always said; use fresh ones for colour and dried ones for depth of flavour.

As well as sambals and pastes, you will find recipes for condiments to complement your meal. The Pickled Green Chillies (page 41) are great with wontons, and the Red Chilli and Ginger Dip (page 41) is perfect for chicken and rice.

Turn to pages 36–37 to see how the pastes, sambals and condiments look and once you have made up a batch, they can sit in your fridge to await your magic touch.

REMPAH KARI
1. CURRY PASTE

Makes 180–200g

20 dried red Kashmiri chillies

7 small, round shallots (185–190g),
  peeled and chopped

4 fresh red chillies, chopped

3 candlenuts or macadamia nuts
  (optional)

1 tsp ground coriander

1 tsp ground cumin

½ tsp turmeric

100ml vegetable oil, plus extra to
  loosen the paste, if necessary

2 stalks fresh curry leaves, leaves
  stripped

2 tsp chicken stock powder

Malaysian curries are fragrant and light compared to their Indian counterparts. This curry paste takes in influences from many different cultures and is a wonderful base to any curry.

Bring some water to the boil in a small saucepan. Add the dried chillies and boil for 5 minutes, then remove from the heat. Leave the chillies to sit in the hot water for at least 15 minutes to soften while you prepare the other ingredients for the spice paste.

Place the chopped shallots in a blender and blitz until smooth. Add the chopped fresh red chillies to the blender.

Once the dried chillies have softened, drain and split them lengthways. Remove the seeds with the blade of your knife and discard. Cut the deseeded dried chillies in half and add them to the blender. Add the candlenuts or macadamia nuts, if using, the ground coriander, cumin and turmeric and blitz all the ingredients until you have a smooth paste. If the paste is too dry, add some oil to loosen it a little.

Heat the oil in a wok or heavy-based frying pan over a medium heat and add the paste, using a spatula to make sure you scrape all of the paste out of the blender. Let the paste heat up slowly, to prevent the paste burning and spitting. Once it sizzles, add the curry leaves and fry, stirring occasionally so that it doesn't stick to the bottom of the wok, for about 30 minutes, or until the oil separates from the paste, then add the chicken stock powder.

TIPS: The paste will keep in a sealed container in the fridge for up to 3 weeks. It can also be frozen.

REMPAH LAKSA
2. LAKSA PASTE

Makes 180–200g

8 dried red Kashmiri chillies

25g dried shrimps

4 small, round shallots, peeled and
    roughly chopped

4 lemongrass stalks (tender base
    only), roughly chopped

30g galangal, peeled and roughly
    chopped

30g ginger, peeled and roughly
    chopped

4 garlic cloves

1 tbsp turmeric

2 tbsp shrimp paste (belacan)

6 candlenuts or macadamia nuts

2 tbsp vegetable oil, plus 5 tbsp for
    frying the paste

There are a few types of laksa in Malaysia and this paste is used to make Nyonya Curry Laksa (page 115). The secret ingredient is dried shrimps, which add such depth. Once fried, this paste will keep in the fridge for up to one month. You can omit the dried shrimps for a vegetarian version, substituting them with dried porcini stock so you don't lose the umami taste.

Bring some water to the boil in a small saucepan. Add the dried chillies and boil for 5 minutes, then remove from the heat. Leave the chillies to sit in the hot water for at least 15 minutes to soften while you prepare the other ingredients for the spice paste.

Place the dried shrimps in a heat-proof bowl, cover with boiling water and leave to rehydrate for 5 minutes. Drain and set aside.

Once the dried chillies have softened, drain and split them lengthways. Remove the seeds with the blade of your knife and discard. Cut the deseeded chillies in half.

Place all of the spice paste ingredients, including the rehydrated chillies and shrimps, in a blender, and blitz to make a smooth paste.

Heat the oil in a wok or heavy-based frying pan over a medium heat and add the paste, using a spatula to make sure you scrape all of the paste out of the blender. Reduce the heat to low and fry the paste for about 15 minutes, stirring with a spatula, until the mixture darkens and the oil separates from the paste (a film of oil will appear at the base of the pan). Your paste is now ready.

TIP: Don't throw away the tops of the lemongrass stalks: freeze them or use them to add to your G&T (page 237).

SAMBAL BELACAN
3. SHRIMP PASTE SAMBAL

Makes 5–7 tablespoons

4 large fresh red chillies, roughly
   chopped (no need to deseed)
juice of 1 lime
1 tsp shrimp paste (belacan)
1 tbsp caster sugar

Sambal belacan is a common Malaysian chilli-based dip. Belacan is shrimp paste, which gives the dip its umami essence and saltiness. My version is slightly lighter than most, so it's suitable to use in salads as well as for dipping.

Place all the ingredients in a small blender and blend until you have a smooth paste. The paste will keep in a sealed container in the fridge for up to 5 days.

SAMBAL KAMPUNG
4. VILLAGE SAMBAL

Makes 400g

10 dried red Kashmiri chillies
75g dried shrimps
8 small, round shallots, roughly
   chopped
3 garlic cloves
4 fresh red chillies, roughly chopped
1 lemongrass stalk (tender base
   only), roughly chopped
5g galangal, roughly chopped
½ tsp turmeric
½ tbsp shrimp paste (belacan)
60ml water
2 tbsp vegetable oil
1 medium ripe tomato, thinly sliced
½ medium onion, diced
2 tbsp tamarind concentrate
1 tbsp caster sugar
¾ tsp salt

The addition of tomatoes and tamarind to this sambal make it lovely and fruity. It's a brilliant accompaniment to vegetables, rice, noodles and even cheese!

Place all the ingredients in a small blender and blend until you have a smooth paste. The paste will keep in a sealed container in the fridge for up to 5 days.

SAMBAL IKAN BILIS
5. ANCHOVY SAMBAL

Makes 300g

12 dried red Kashmiri chillies
50g good-quality dried anchovies
10 small, round shallots, peeled and
    roughly chopped
7 fresh red chillies, roughly chopped
2 lemongrass stalks (tender base
    only), roughly chopped
2 garlic cloves
½ tbsp shrimp paste
150ml vegetable oil
3–4 tbsp tamarind concentrate
½ tsp salt
¾ tbsp caster sugar
1 tbsp chicken stock powder

This is my favourite sambal and it's essential if you want to make Nasi Lemak (page 107). It is both sweet and spicy, with the dried anchovies (ikan bilis) adding saltiness and the tamarind making it tangy. Combined with coconut rice, it is just perfect, but it's great as a dip for raw vegetables too. It keeps well in a sealed container in the fridge for up to four weeks and can be frozen.

Bring some water to the boil in a small saucepan. Add the dried chillies and boil for 5 minutes, then remove from the heat. Leave the chillies to sit in the hot water for at least 15 minutes to soften while you prepare the other ingredients.

Place the dried anchovies in a heat-proof bowl, cover with hot water and leave to soak for 15 minutes

Place the chopped shallots in a blender and blitz until smooth. Add the chopped fresh red chillies to the blender.

Once the dried chillies have softened, drain and split them lengthways. Remove the seeds with the blade of your knife and discard. Cut the deseeded dried chillies in half and add them to the blender.

Add the lemongrass, garlic and shrimp paste and blitz until you have a smooth paste. Loosen with some of the vegetable oil if the paste is too dry.

Heat the oil in a wok or heavy-based frying pan over a medium heat and add the paste. Reduce the heat to low and fry the paste for about 20 minutes, stirring with a spatula to make sure the mixture doesn't stick to the bottom of the pan, until the oil separates from the paste. Add the tamarind, salt, sugar and chicken stock powder, and leave to cool at room temperature, before transferring it to an airtight container and storing in the fridge.

TIP: To freeze the sambal, place a double layer of cling film on the work surface and spoon the cooled sambal onto it to form a sausage. Roll the cling film up, enclosing the sambal, and twist the ends to seal. Place in the freezer. Cut off portions of the frozen paste as and when you need it.

MINYAK BAWANG PUTIH
6. GARLIC OIL

Makes 4 tablespoons

4 tbsp vegetable or other
   flavourless oil
4 fat garlic cloves, as finely and
   evenly chopped as possible

This is one of my go-to essentials. It is so simple to make yet adds a great flavour to a lot of dishes and keeps for up to two weeks at room temperature.

Heat the oil in a frying pan over a medium heat for about 1 minute. Drop the chopped garlic into the pan. Swirl the pan so that the garlic is evenly distributed. As soon as the garlic changes colour from white to light golden, remove the pan from the heat immediately and set it aside. The garlic will continue to cook and will turn a rich golden colour. Transfer the oil and garlic to a ramekin or glass jar.

TIP: Do not use olive oil, or any other flavoured oil.

SOS CILI MANIS DAN DAUN SELASIH THAI
7. THAI BASIL AND SWEET CHILLI DIP

Makes 6 tablespoons

6 tbsp sweet chilli sauce
1 tbsp rice wine or white wine
   vinegar
2 tbsp cold water
4 sprigs of Thai basil, leaves
   stripped
1 garlic clove

This is my mum's invention as she was too lazy one day to make a chilli dip from scratch for the Caramel Pork Belly with Soy (page 132), so instead she threw things together that she had in the fridge and pantry and, hey presto, it is now one of the family's favourite dips.

Mix the sweet chilli sauce, vinegar and water together. Chop the basil leaves and garlic finely and add them to the chilli mixture. Serve immediately.

SOS KICAP DAN CILI PADI
8. BIRD'S-EYE CHILLI AND SOY DIP

Serves 4

8 red or green bird's eye chillies,
   finely chopped
4 tbsp light soy sauce, plus extra
   if needed

This super-simple condiment is served with almost every noodle dish in Malaysia. It is important to use bird's eye chillies, as the flavour of the little devils is more potent and flavoursome than bigger chillies. I especially love dipping pork bones from the Simple Pork and Anchovy Broth (page 85) in it and greedily stripping them bare.

Divide the chopped chillies between 4 small dipping bowls.
   Add 1 tablespoon of the soy sauce to each bowl, or enough to cover the chopped chilli. Using the back of a small spoon, lightly crush the chillies to release their flavour. Serve immediately.

TIP: Fresh chillies freeze well and defrost in minutes, so it's worth buying them in bulk.

JERUK BAWANG MERAH
9. PICKLED SHALLOTS

Serves about 4 as an
accompaniment

4 small, round shallots, peeled,
   thinly sliced and separated into
   individual rings
4 tsp caster sugar
100ml rice wine vinegar

This pickle goes with anything rich that needs lightening up and is lovely with the Malaysian Flaky Bread Stuffed with Spiced Lamb (page 71). And an added bonus is that it's easy to make and keeps well.

Place the shallots in a glass jar or ramekin.
   Put the sugar and vinegar in a bowl and mix until all the sugar has dissolved.
   Pour the sugar-vinegar mixture over the shallots. Leave the shallots to pickle for at least 2 hours before using. Cover and store in the fridge until needed. The shallots keep for up to 1 week, but they're so good they won't last long!

KUAH KACANG
10. PEANUT SAUCE

Makes around 650g (serves 6–8 as an accompaniment)

300g salted peanuts
12g dried red chillies (about 20 chillies)
½ onion, roughly chopped
2 garlic cloves
20g ginger, peeled and roughly chopped
3 lemongrass stalks (tender base only), roughly chopped
6 tbsp vegetable oil
5 tbsp tamarind concentrate
3½ tbsp caster sugar
1½ tsp salt
400ml water
2 tbsp dark sweet soy sauce
120ml coconut milk

This is often served as an accompaniment for satay. To me, a delicious peanut sauce is creamy (without being sickly), spicy, sweet and sour all at the same time. The sauce can be frozen so make a big batch. It's delicious with any grilled meats and salads like Gado-Gado (page 80).

Put the peanuts in a blender or the bowl of a food processor, and blitz until coarsely chopped. Remove and set aside.

Bring some water to the boil in a small saucepan. Add the dried chillies and boil for 5 minutes, then remove from the heat. Leave the chillies to sit in the hot water for at least 15 minutes to soften.

Once the dried chillies have softened, drain and split them lengthways. Remove the seeds with the blade of your knife and discard. Cut the deseeded dried chillies into pieces and add them to the blender or processor with the onion, garlic, ginger and bottom halves of the lemongrass stalks. Blitz until you have a smooth paste, adding some of the vegetable oil if necessary, to loosen the paste.

Heat the oil in a wok or heavy-based frying pan over a medium heat and scrape the paste into the pan with a spatula. Fry the paste for about 5 minutes, until fragrant.

Add the tamarind concentrate, 2 of the bruised lemongrass tips, sugar and salt. Cook gently for 5–8 minutes until the oil separates and it turns darker in colour (be careful not to burn the mixture).

Add the chopped peanuts, water, soy sauce and coconut milk. Reduce the heat and cook for 20–30 minutes, stirring, until the sauce thickens. Check from time to time that the sauce isn't sticking to the base of the pan. Adjust the seasoning if necessary: a good peanut sauce should be spicy, sweet, sour and creamy.

JERUK CILI HIJAU
11. PICKLED GREEN CHILLIES

Fills 1 x 250g jar

1 tsp salt
165g fresh green chillies, cut into
  0.5cm thick slices
6 tsp caster sugar
250ml distilled white vinegar

I adore pickled green chillies and I first tried them when I was a child. My mum loved them with wontons, so she would always ask for extra from the street vendors.

To sterilise the jar, either boil it in a saucepan of water for 5 minutes, put it through a dishwasher cycle or heat it in the oven (preheated to 150°C/130°C fan/300°F/Gas 2) for 10 minutes.

Bring a saucepan of water to the boil, add the salt and blanch the sliced chillies for 1 minute. Drain thoroughly and transfer the chillies to a bowl of ice-cold water to stop them cooking.

Put the sugar in the sterilised jar with the vinegar and stir to dissolve the sugar, then drain the chillies and add them to the jar. The pickled chillies will be ready to eat the next day, but can be kept in a cool, dark place for up to 6 weeks.

SOS CILI MERAH DAN HALIA
12. RED CHILLI AND GINGER DIP

Makes 100–120g

4 fresh red chillies, roughly chopped
25g ginger, peeled and roughly
  chopped
2 garlic cloves
2 tbsp water
grated zest and juice of 1 lime
1½ tsp caster sugar
large pinch of salt

This spicy, tangy and moreish dipping sauce is very versatile. I love mixing it with meatballs and white rice, but it's also great with chicken, pork and noodle dishes. It keeps for up to four days in a sealed container in the fridge.

Place the chillies, ginger, garlic and water in a small blender and blitz until smooth.

Place the chilli mixture in a small saucepan over a low heat.

Add the lime zest and juice, sugar and salt, and cook gently until the sugar has completely dissolved. If it is too thick, loosen it with a little water.

Simmer for 2 minutes then remove from heat. Leave to cool, and it is ready to use.

SOS PLUM DAN SRIRACHA

13. PLUM AND SRIRACHA SAUCE

Makes about 230ml

5 tbsp sriracha chilli sauce
5 tbsp clear plum sauce
1 tbsp sesame seeds

I use sriracha a lot but needed to make it sweeter for my Cucur Udang (page 46), and had this bottle of plum sauce sitting in my pantry, so I added it to the sriracha and it worked a treat. It goes well with the Five-spice Pork Spring Rolls (page 50) too.

Mix the sriracha and plum sauce together in a mixing bowl. Sprinkle with sesame seeds.

MINYAK HEBI
14. SHRIMP CHILLI OIL

Makes 2 × 500g jars

50g dried red Kashmiri chillies
100g dried shrimps
50g small, round shallots, peeled
    and roughly chopped
300ml vegetable oil, plus extra for
    topping up the jars
1 tbsp chicken stock powder
½ tbsp caster sugar

This is great with soft-boiled eggs (page 66) and essential in my Chilli Pan Mee (page 111). It keeps well for up to one month and makes a lovely gift.

Bring some water to the boil in a small saucepan. Add the dried chillies and boil for 5 minutes, then remove from the heat. Leave the chillies to sit in the hot water for at least 15 minutes to soften.

Meanwhile, place the dried shrimps in a heat-proof bowl and cover them with boiling water. Leave to rehydrate for 5 minutes, then drain and grind coarsely in a blender. Remove and set aside.

Once the dried chillies have softened, drain and split them lengthways. Remove the seeds with the blade of your knife and discard. Cut the deseeded dried chillies in half and add them to the blender.

Add the shallots to the blender and blitz – the paste doesn't need to be too smooth.

Heat the oil in a wok or heavy-based frying pan over a medium heat and add the shallot and chilli paste. Warm through, then add the shrimps. Fry over a low–medium heat for 20–25 minutes, until fragrant and the oil separates from the paste. The colour will darken significantly. Add the chicken stock powder and sugar then remove from the heat and leave to cool, then spoon into sterilised jars until three-quarters full and top up the jars with vegetable oil. Seal and store in a cool, dark place until ready to use.

SMALL PLATES
AND SNACKS

We eat little and often in Malaysia, on average about five times a day, and we talk about food all day long, planning what to eat about two meals ahead of time. So it comes as no surprise that we have a huge variety of foods. In Malaysia, we wouldn't tend to make most of the dishes in this chapter at home, as they can be bought so easily and cheaply from street food vendors. The quality does vary from stall to stall, but the good ones sell out in a flash.

I've included some of the country's best-loved dishes, such as Malaysian Prawn Fritters (Alexa's favourite – page 46) and tender Chicken Satay (page 49) marinated in lemongrass, turmeric and cumin, served with a spicy and sweet peanut sauce.

Since I moved to the UK, I have had to learn how to make the snacks I grew up with, and to improvise where necessary, while preserving the tastes I remember from my childhood. Some of the dishes are well-known Malaysian street foods, some are my mum's secret recipes and some are more modern interpretations of Malaysian flavours. They are usually served in small portions, making them suitable for party food or starters.

CUCUR UDANG

MALAYSIAN PRAWN FRITTERS

Makes 25–30 fritters

150g plain flour
125g self-raising flour
1 tsp salt
1 tbsp chicken stock powder
1 tsp caster sugar
1 tsp turmeric
¼ tsp ground white pepper
375ml cold water
6 garlic chives (kuchai) or spring
    onions, cut into 3cm lengths
300g raw king prawns, peeled and
    kept whole
400ml vegetable oil, for deep-frying

Cucur is a well-known street food in Malaysia. It's very easy to make and can be eaten either hot or at room temperature. The accompanying dip varies, depending on where in Malaysia you are from. They are delicious with either Plum and Sriracha Sauce (page 42) or Peanut Sauce (page 40), or simply dipped in sweet chilli sauce. They should be crispy on the outside, soft and pillowy inside.

Put all the dry ingredients in a large mixing bowl. Gradually whisk in the water to make a batter (it shouldn't be too lumpy, and should coat the back of a spoon). Add the chives or spring onions, and the prawns. Set the batter aside to rest or 5–10 minutes.

Heat the oil in a small saucepan. It should be hot enough that when you drop a tiny bit of batter in, it sizzles and quickly floats to the surface (it should be about 180°C).

Using a metal dessertspoon, carefully drop a dollop of the batter into the oil, making sure there are prawns and chives in the spoonful of mixture. It should float to the surface pretty quickly. Repeat with more batter, but don't overcrowd the pan (cook in batches if necessary). Fry for 3–4 minutes, turning the fritters occasionally with a pair of chopsticks or tongs to ensure they are evenly cooked. Remove with a slotted spoon and drain on kitchen paper.

Serve with Plum and Sriracha Sauce or a dipping sauce of your choice.

TIPS: The fritters can be made up to 2 hours in advance, so they're great for parties. If you want them hot, warm them through in a 180°C/ 160°C fan/350°F/Gas 4 oven for about 5 minutes.

If you want to make the fritters go further, chop up the prawns and make the dollops of batter smaller. Cook them for a shorter amount of time. However, keeping the prawns whole looks better and they keep moist and juicy.

SATAY AYAM
CHICKEN SATAY

Makes 10–15 skewers

300g boneless chicken thighs, skin on (you can take it off if you prefer, but it helps keep the chicken moist), cut into strips about 2cm thick
Peanut Sauce (page 40), to serve

For the marinade
3 lemongrass stalks (tender base only)
2 tbsp coconut milk (optional)
1 tbsp turmeric
¼ tbsp ground cumin
1 tsp salt
1 tsp caster sugar
1 tsp vegetable oil

Satay is probably the most well-known dish of Malaysia. The chicken is cooked slowly on an open charcoal fire and, to keep the meat moist, chicken fat is added between the chunks of meat, and brushed with coconut milk. They are always cooked to order but worth the wait. This recipe goes beautifully with Peanut Sauce (page 40).

Blitz the lemongrass to make roughly 2 tablespoons of lemongrass purée. Soak 10–15 bamboo skewers in water overnight (to prevent them burning during cooking). Place the chicken strips in a bowl with the marinade ingredients (including the lemongrass purée), stir to coat, cover and leave to marinate in the fridge overnight (or for at least for 4 hours).

Thread the marinated chicken pieces onto the soaked skewers.

Heat a griddle pan or a grill and gently grill the chicken for about 4 minutes, until cooked through. Keep turning the skewers to ensure they are evenly cooked. Alternatively, cook on the barbecue and they will have a lovely charred surface.

Serve with peanut sauce.

TIP: For a more substantial meal, keep the chicken thighs whole and serve with rice or salad.

LOR BAK
FIVE-SPICE PORK SPRING ROLLS

Makes 5 fat spring rolls

300g pork loin, cut into thin strips
    (about 1cm thick)
2 tsp five-spice powder
1 tbsp tapioca flour or cornflour
1 medium free-range egg
½ tsp chicken stock powder
½ red onion, chopped
5 water chestnuts, roughly chopped
5 × 22cm spring roll sheets
500ml vegetable oil, for deep-frying

For the marinade

2 tbsp caster sugar
½ tsp salt
2 large pinches of ground white
    pepper
1 tsp chicken stock powder

A 'coffee shop' in Malaysia usually consists of several stalls selling their specialty, so there is a variety of food on offer. There is a coffee shop near my old house in Ipoh where I always order the *lor bak* from a sweet old man who deep-fries them to crisp up the skin. Traditionally they are wrapped with bean curd skins but I use spring roll sheets as they are easier to find and store.

Place the pork strips in a bowl with the marinade ingredients, stir to coat, cover and leave to marinate in the fridge overnight.

The next day, discard the water that has come out of the pork. Mix the marinated pork with the five-spice powder, tapioca flour or cornflour, egg and chicken stock powder. Add the chopped onion and chestnuts. Mix well.

Place 1 of the spring roll sheets on a flat work surface in front of you, positioning it so that you have a diamond shape. Place some of the pork mixture horizontally 4cm up from the bottom of the sheet. Fold the bottom up over the mixture, fold in the 2 sides and roll up tightly, brushing the edges with water as you go. Place the spring roll on a plate and transfer it to the fridge for 30 minutes to firm up. Repeat with the remaining spring roll sheets and pork mixture.

Heat the oil in a wok or a wide saucepan until it reaches 180°C on a probe thermometer. Alternatively, drop a tiny bit of spring roll sheet into the oil to test if the oil is hot enough: the spring roll sheet should sizzle vigorously and quickly float to the top.

Deep-fry the spring rolls in batches of 2 or 3 at a time, for 8–10 minutes over a medium heat, until golden brown (too high a heat will burn the outside and leave the middle raw), then transfer to kitchen paper to drain.

Slice the spring rolls diagonally and serve with Plum and Sriracha Sauce (page 42) for dipping.

TIP: If you use a wok, you can fry more spring rolls at a time (as the surface area is wider).

SANG CHOI PAU

SPICY MINCED CHICKEN AND LEMONGRASS PARCELS

Serves 4–6

50g glass noodles

2 tbsp vegetable oil

3 garlic cloves, finely chopped

2 bird's eye chillies, finely chopped

2 lemongrass stalks (tender base only), finely chopped

10 green beans, finely chopped

1 medium carrot, finely chopped

150g minced chicken

150g raw peeled king prawns, roughly chopped

1½ tbsp oyster sauce

1 tbsp fish sauce

½ tsp rice wine vinegar

1 iceberg lettuce or 2 Little Gem lettuces, leaves separated

150g salted roast peanuts, coarsely crushed

lime wedges, to serve

freshly ground black or white pepper

The first time I had a dish like this was in London, in a restaurant called Hunan. I remember the owner, Mr Peng, called this a chicken sandwich. It was crunchy, spicy and wonderful. As you will see, this doesn't look like a sandwich, but I get where he is going with this. In Cantonese it is called *sang choi pau*, which essentially means 'lettuce wrap'. These little gems are crunchy and spicy, are easy to make and fun to eat.

Put the glass noodles in a heat-proof bowl, cover with boiling water and leave to soak for 5 minutes. Drain and rinse under cold running water. Cut them into little pieces with scissors and set aside.

Heat the oil in a wok or large frying pan, then add the garlic, chillies and lemongrass and stir-fry for about 1 minute until fragrant, then add green beans and carrot. Stir-fry for 2 minutes, until the vegetables lose their rawness but maintain a crunch.

Add the minced chicken and break it up while mixing it with the vegetables. Once the chicken turns opaque and starts to cook through, add the prawns. Add the oyster sauce and fish sauce. Season with pepper and cook for a further 1–2 minutes, then add the snipped noodles and mix well. Cook for a further minute then make sure the chicken and prawns are cooked. Add the rice wine vinegar, mix well and take the wok or pan off the heat. Set aside and leave to cool for 10 minutes.

To prepare the lettuce, use scissors to follow the curve of the leaves and cut away the green floppy parts, leaving just a firmer section, which acts like a cup. Spoon the mixture into the lettuce cups and sprinkle liberally with crushed peanuts. Squeeze a little lime juice on top of the mince before eating.

TIPS: If iceberg lettuce is too fiddly, Little Gem leaves are firmer yet make slightly smaller parcels.

Other toppings like crushed prawn crackers, crispy shallots and Shrimp Chilli Oil (page 43) work well too.

MUM'S CHICKEN WINGS

Makes 12 wings

12 large chicken wings
60g peeled ginger
2 garlic cloves
2 tbsp water
2 tbsp oyster sauce
1 tbsp dark soy sauce (optional, but
   it gives them a rich, dark colour)
1 tsp caster sugar
½ tsp English mustard

My mum's chicken wings are legendary. She often makes them when we have a family barbecue, knowing that they are my favourite. The wings can be cooked under the grill or on the barbecue, but I tend to use the oven. The key to delicious wings is to marinate them, preferably the day before you want to eat them, giving them a good massage to coat them thoroughly before putting them in the fridge.

Place the chicken wings in a ziplock bag or a roasting tray.

Place the ginger and garlic in a blender or the bowl of a small food processor with the water and blitz to a smooth paste.

Place the remaining ingredients in the blender or processor and pulse until well incorporated.

Pour the marinade over the chicken wings and give them a good rub to makes sure that the wings are completely coated with the marinade.

Seal the bag or cover the tray and marinate the wings overnight in the fridge, or for at least 4 hours.

Preheat the oven to 180°C/160°C fan/350°F/Gas 4. Place the marinated wings on a roasting tray and cook for 25 minutes, or until cooked through and dark brown.

TIP: If you have a probe thermometer to check that the wings are cooked through, the temperature in the thickest part of the wings should reach at least 74°C.

LOBAK YUN

PAN-FRIED PORK PATTIES
WITH MOOLI AND DRIED SHRIMPS

Makes about 15 patties

300g mooli (about 1 whole medium
    one), peeled and grated
40g dried shrimps
350g minced pork (not lean)
3 tbsp cornflour
1 tbsp chicken stock powder
½ tsp caster sugar
¼ tsp ground white pepper
1 tbsp vegetable oil
Red Chilli and Ginger Dip, to serve
    (page 41)

The mooli radish is also known as 'lobak' in Malaysia and
'daikon' in Japan. Back home, my mum makes the most
delicious 'lobak balls' that are flavoured with mooli, pork and
dried shrimps and it's her recipe that has inspired this dish.
I have adapted it using ingredients available here in the UK
that retain the essence and flavour of her dish.

Bring a pan of water to the boil, add the grated mooli and cook
for 10 minutes. Drain, wrap the mooli in muslin and squeeze
out all the excess water. Set aside.

Place the dried shrimps in a heat-proof bowl, cover with
boiling water, and leave to rehydrate for 5 minutes. Drain and
finely chop.

In a mixing bowl, combine the minced pork, shrimps and
mooli with the remaining ingredients (except the oil). Mix well
with your hands, then cover and leave to marinate in the fridge
for at least 2 hours.

Shape the pork mixture into about 15 golf-ball sized balls,
then flatten them slightly.

Heat the oil in a non-stick frying pan. Gently fry the patties
for about 3 minutes on each side until cooked through.

Serve with Red Chilli and Ginger Dip.

KULIT AYAM GORENG
DEEP-FRIED CHICKEN SKIN

Makes 6–9 pieces

3 large chicken legs
6 tbsp plain flour
1 tsp garlic powder
1 tsp onion powder
1 tsp Malaysian curry powder or any
    mild curry powder
1 tsp chicken stock powder
½ tsp salt
300ml vegetable oil, for deep-frying
4 tbsp milk
Maggi Chilli Sauce (or chilli sauce of
    your choice), to serve

On Gurney Drive, a famous street food promenade in Malaysia, I came across a stall with slithers of deep-fried 'something' and when I found out they were chicken skins, I got giddy – it was SO bad, but so GOOD. I have never forgotten it, so here is my recreation of that naughtiness.

Carefully remove the skin from the chicken legs. Cut each piece of skin into 2–3 pieces, depending on how large they are. Using the blade of a knife, scrape away the excess fat. Lay the skin flat on a plate or tray.

Combine the flour, garlic powder, onion powder, curry powder, chicken stock powder and salt and transfer the mixture to a plate.

Heat the oil in a small saucepan to 180°C.

Dip a piece of skin in milk, drain off the excess, then put it straight onto the flour mixture. Shake it a bit to remove the excess flour. Repeat with the remaining pieces of skin.

Once the oil is hot enough, carefully drop in the skin, making sure it stays open and doesn't crumple (I hold the skin apart with my metal tongs for the initial 20 seconds of frying). Do not overcrowd the pan (fry in batches if necessary). Fry for 2–3 minutes until golden, turning down the heat if it is too hot.

Serve with Maggi Chilli Sauce.

TIP: Debone the chicken legs after you've skinned them, and mince the meat to make a Spicy Minced Chicken and Lemongrass Parcel (page 52) or slice the meat for a mid-week stir-fry.

TELUR KOPITIAM

KOPITIAM EGGS

Serves 2

4 medium free-range eggs (I use
    Clarence Court)
1 tsp light soy sauce
ground white pepper
buttered toast or Kaya French Toast
    (page 216), to serve

Kopitiam in Malaysia means 'coffee shop', and I grew up eating these eggs there. I love the combination of light soy sauce and white pepper with the coddled eggs – they really complement the sweetness of the kaya toast. Use standard ground white pepper, as the more expensive stuff doesn't give the right taste. Serve these on buttered toast – which is how some *kopitiam* serve them – and they'll become 'telur goyang', meaning 'eggs that move as they wobble'.

Bring a saucepan of water to a rolling boil. Make sure the water is deep enough to cover the eggs. Turn off the heat and place the eggs in the water. Leave for 6 minutes.

Crack 2 eggs into a bowl or onto a piece of toast.

Season with ½ a teaspoon of soy sauce and a pinch of ground white pepper and serve with buttered toast or Kaya French Toast (page 216).

ACHAR AWAK
SPICY PICKLED VEGETABLES

Fills 3 × 500ml jars

2 cucumbers, quartered lengthways,
    deseeded, and cut into batons
2½ tbsp salt
330g cabbage (about ¾ of a whole
    cabbage), cored and cut into
    3cm chunks
3 medium carrots, quartered
    lengthways then cut into
    3cm lengths
200g green beans, cut into
    3cm lengths
165g caster sugar
1 tsp chicken stock powder
5 tbsp white vinegar
150ml vegetable oil
100g honey roasted peanuts,
    crushed, to serve

For blanching the vegetables
600ml water
2 tbsp caster sugar
½ tbsp salt
200ml white vinegar

For the spice paste
20 dried red Kashmiri chillies
8 small round shallots, peeled
    and chopped
5 fresh red chillies

1 tsp turmeric
1 lemongrass stalk (tender base
    only), roughly chopped
3 candlenuts or macadamia nuts
    (optional)
1 tsp shrimp paste (belacan)

It might seem like a lot of veg, but it is worth making the entire recipe, as it can be kept in the fridge in sealed jars for two weeks. It is delicious eaten on its own with an aperitif or as an accompaniment to a main course.

Place the cucumber batons in a colander, mix with 1 tablespoon of salt, set the colander over a bowl and leave for at least 30 minutes. The salt will draw out the moisture. Press lightly on the cucumber to squeeze out as much water as possible into the bowl below.

Place the water for blanching the vegetables in a saucepan with the sugar, remaining salt and vinegar, and bring to the boil. Blanch the vegetables 1 at a time: 10 seconds for the cucumber, 20 seconds for the cabbage, and 30 seconds for the carrots and beans. Drain the blanched vegetables and transfer them to a bowl of ice-cold water to stop the cooking process.

For the spice paste, bring some water to the boil in a small saucepan, add the dried chillies and boil for 5 minutes, then remove them from the heat. Leave the chillies to sit in the hot water for at least 15 minutes to soften, while you prepare the other ingredients for the spice paste. Place the chopped shallots in a blender and blitz until smooth. Add the chopped fresh red chillies to the blender. Once the dried chillies have softened, drain and split them lengthways. Remove the seeds with the blade of your knife and discard. Cut the deseeded dried chillies in half and add them to the blender.

Place all the remaining ingredients for the spice paste in the blender and blitz until you have a smooth paste.

Heat the oil in a wok or heavy-based frying pan over a medium heat and add the paste, using a spatula to make sure you scrape all of the paste out of the blender. Let the paste heat up slowly, to prevent it burning, and sizzle gently. Fry for 5–10 minutes until it is fragrant. If it starts to stick to the bottom of the wok, turn down the heat. Add the sugar, remaining salt and chicken stock powder. Bring to the boil then remove from the heat. Leave to cool and stir in the vinegar. Add the vegetables, cover and leave to marinate in the fridge overnight.

To serve, sprinkle the crushed honey-roasted peanuts on top.

BAWANG PERAI SAMBAL KAMPUNG
CHARRED LEEKS WITH SAMBAL KAMPUNG

Serves 4

4 large leeks
2 tbsp vegetable oil
1 tbsp rock salt
Sambal Kampung (page 34),
   to serve

There is a growing trend for charring vegetables, and the subtle smokiness this imparts makes them incredibly seductive, adding another dimension to the vegetables. Traditionally, Sambal Kampung is served with blanched vegetables like okra or aubergine, but you can eat it with raw vegetables too. By charring the leeks, I wanted to add a touch of modernity to accompany the traditional *sambal* and it works a treat.

Coat the leeks generously with vegetable oil and salt.

Place the leeks on the barbecue or in a griddle pan (over a medium–low heat) and grill for about 20–30 minutes, until the outside of the leeks are burnt and the insides are soft (the cooking time will depend on the size of the leeks).

Don't worry that the outer layer of the leeks is burnt. Once the leeks are cooked through, you peel the burnt layer off and eat the soft fleshy bits in the middle. The outer layer acts as protection from the heat and the charring adds smokiness. Serve with generous dollops of Sambal Kampung.

KARI POPCORN
CURRY POPCORN

Serves 2

2 tsp vegetable oil
25g corn kernels
2 tsp caster sugar
20g butter
½ tsp Malaysian curry powder
  or Madras curry powder
½ tsp fennel seeds, slightly crushed
pinch of salt

My husband Andrew is obsessed with popcorn. Every time we go to the cinema, he'll buy some, regardless of how full he is. After becoming my 'development chef and chief critic', he started to make gourmet popcorn at home. So this is his creation, with a little input from me, and I have to say it's pretty yummy. It is sweet and savoury at the same time, so your first mouthful takes a while to register the flavours and then it becomes seriously moreish.

Heat the oil in a medium saucepan over a medium heat. Add the corn kernels and cover. The corn will soon start to pop. Continue cooking, with the lid firmly on the pan, until the popping slows down and you can count a few seconds in between pops.

Turn off the heat, remove the lid and immediately sprinkle the sugar over the hot corn. Stir the popcorn in the pan to gently melt the sugar and coat the kernels.

Melt the butter in a small frying pan or separate saucepan, add the curry powder and crushed fennel seeds, and fry for around 30 seconds, until the butter starts to foam.

While turning the corn in the pan, trickle the spiced butter over the corn until it is all coated.

Turn the corn out into a serving bowl and sprinkle over some salt.

SMALL PLATES AND SNACKS

SOFT-BOILED EGGS WITH SHRIMP CHILLI OIL

Serves 2–4

2 medium free-range eggs, at room
    temperature
2 tbsp Shrimp Chilli Oil (page 43)

One day I came home starving to find that all I had was eggs
and chilli oil, so this recipe was born. Soft-boiled eggs are my
favourite and eating them with shrimp chilli oil is just the
best snack.

Bring a saucepan of water to the boil. Lower the eggs in with a
spoon. Boil for 6 minutes, remove and drop them into ice-cold
water to stop the cooking process.

When cool, peel away the shells and halve the eggs
lengthways. The yolks should still be runny. Drizzle the Shrimp
Chilli Oil over the eggs (a light drizzle, or a heavy dolloping for
the hard core).

TIP: Use good-quality eggs for this dish as you want rich,
runny yolks. I used Burford Brown or Cornish Legbar eggs.

ROTI CANAI
FLAKY BREAD

Makes 6 rotis

85ml water
50ml condensed milk
1 medium free-range egg
¾ tsp salt
1 tbsp vegetable oil, plus extra for
    greasing and covering
300g plain flour

In my humble opinion this soft, flaky and slightly sweet bread is the best flatbread ever. If you are ever in Malaysia, visit the Mamak stalls where you can see this bread being made. They flip it with their hands until it has tripled in size, then it is folded to trap the air, and griddled to order. We usually eat this for breakfast, but to be honest you can eat *roti* at any time of day.

Beat the water, condensed milk, egg, salt and oil together until they are well incorporated. Pour 50ml of the batter into another bowl and set aside in case you need it later.

Sift the flour into another bowl and make a well in the centre. Slowly pour in the liquid mixture, incorporating it into the flour as you go, until the dough comes together. The dough will seem a little sticky at first but after kneading for 5 minutes, it will become smooth. Don't be tempted to add extra flour. Leave the dough to rest for at least 20 minutes, covered, then knead for another 5 minutes. Divide the dough into 6 balls. Coat your hands in vegetable oil and coat the dough balls.

Put the balls in a shallow container in which they fit snugly. Pour over enough vegetable oil to cover the balls. Cover and leave in the fridge overnight.

The next day, take 1 ball out of the container and place it on a work surface. Press it lightly then stretch it out with the palm of your hand until it's big enough for you to hold with both hands. Put your left hand on top of the dough with your thumb tucked underneath and put your right hand underneath the dough with your thumb on top. Lift the dough up and flip it from your right hand to your left, and then immediately slap it on the surface. Repeat this process 3–4 times. The idea is to stretch it out as thinly as possible.

Fold the 4 corners in towards the middle to form a square, trapping as much air as possible, and put a non-stick frying pan over a medium heat.

Dry-fry the breads on both sides until they are golden brown. Once cooked, put them onto a work surface. Using the palm of your hands scrunch the edges of the warm bread in towards the middle much like clapping your hands with the bread in between. This will give the breads a lovely flakiness.

TIPS: If the dough is too dry, slowly add some of the leftover liquid to create a sticky dough. I find that different brands of flour might need a little more liquid.

The bigger the container you rest the balls of dough in, the more oil you need to cover them. You can reuse the oil though.

SMALL PLATES AND SNACKS

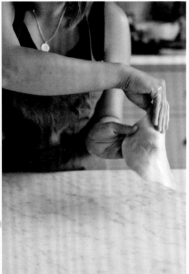

MURTABAK

MALAYSIAN FLAKY BREAD STUFFED WITH SPICED LAMB

Makes 4

4 Malaysian Flaky Bread dough
   balls (page 68)
2 tbsp vegetable oil, plus 1 tsp
1 small onion, diced
1 tsp Malaysian curry powder
   or Madras curry powder
½ tsp garam masala
½ tsp turmeric
300g minced lamb
¾ tsp salt
1 tsp caster sugar
1 tsp light soy sauce
2 eggs, beaten
Pickled Shallots (page 39),
   to serve

The best *murtabak* I have ever had was in Kuala Lumpur near my cousin's house. She took me there many moons ago and I still remember the taste. Crispy bread with flavoursome lamb spilling out when I bit into it, followed by a burst of sourness from the pickled shallots that cut through the richness of the lamb and prepared the palate for another bite.

While the dough is resting (see page 68), make the filling.

Heat 2 tablespoons of the oil in a frying pan and fry the onion until soft, then add the curry powder, garam masala and turmeric (be careful not to burn the spices).

Add the minced lamb and fry until cooked through. Season with the salt, sugar and soy sauce.

Drain the cooked lamb through a sieve to get rid of the excess oil. Set the lamb aside.

Follow the instructions for shaping the dough on page 68. Stretch the dough out to a rectangular shape on a flat work surface to make it as thin as possible, then place 2–3 spoonfuls of beaten egg in the middle, followed by 2–3 spoonfuls of minced lamb.

Fold the dough upwards, fold in the sides and finally the top side of the dough down to form a square parcel.

Heat 1 teaspoon of oil in a non-stick frying pan and transfer the parcel to the pan. Fry until all sides of the dough are golden and crispy. Remove and repeat with the remaining dough balls and filling.

Serve hot or at room temperature with Pickled Shallots.

SALADS AND BROTHS

Salads in Malaysia are more than just a selection of salad leaves; they offer myriad textures and layers of flavours. I recently made Spicy Rice Vermicelli Salad (page 77) for six Italians who hadn't tried Malaysian food before. I was nervous, as they were cooking a huge Puglian meal for us and the salad stood out like a sore thumb. The first mouthful was too spicy for Gianni but then he kept going. It was gone before I knew it. They loved the intense flavours and different textures, and that is what Malaysian salads are all about. They tend to be quite substantial, with the addition of glass or rice noodles, and are either served cold or at room temperature (with the exception of Gado-Gado) and one thing's for sure – they all pack a punch!

For warming my soul, my favourite things in the whole wide world are my mum's broths. Traditionally broths are cooked slowly on a charcoal hob for at least four to six hours. They simmer away over a low heat until all the minerals and nutrients from the bones and meat are released into the broth, creating a pure, delicious nectar. My mum uses pork or chicken bones to make the base. Making broths takes time and love and my mum always tells me it's okay not to eat a big meal when I'm busy, but I absolutely must have broths.

SALAD KARI AYAM PANGGANG
GRILLED CURRY CHICKEN SALAD

Serves 2

For the chicken
2 boneless thighs, skin on
2 tsp Home-made Curry Paste
    (page 32) or shop-bought
2 tbsp coconut milk
pinch of salt and freshly ground
    black pepper

For the crunchy slaw
½ small red cabbage, thickly sliced
juice of 1 lime
1 tsp sesame seeds
pinch of salt and pepper, to taste

For the spiced dressing
4 tbsp crème fraiche
1 tsp home-made Curry Paste
    (page 32) or shop-bought
pinch of salt and freshly ground
    black pepper, to taste

60g brown rice, quinoa or pearl
    barley
1 tsp vegetable oil
coriander and mint leaves, torn,
    to serve
2 lime wedges

Who doesn't love a chicken curry? There are hundreds of variations (I have two recipes in this book alone), but come the summer in the UK, some people might want something a little lighter and this is the perfect recipe for that occasion.

Place the chicken thighs between 2 sheets of cling film and bash them gently with a rolling pin or meat hammer, to flatten them out. This helps to tenderise the meat and makes it quicker to cook. Place the flattened chicken in a bowl with the curry paste, coconut milk and salt and pepper and leave to marinate for at least 30 minutes at room temperature or cover and chill overnight.

Cook the rice, quinoa or pearl barley according to the packet instructions, being careful not to overcook it. The grains should be loose, not clumped together.

Mix all the ingredients for the slaw together in a bowl and set aside.

Mix all the ingredients for the spiced dressing in a bowl and set aside.

To cook the chicken, heat the teaspoon of oil in a griddle or frying pan over a medium heat. Place the chicken skin-side down in the griddle pan and grill or fry for 2–3 minutes or until the skin is crispy. Don't move the chicken while it cooks. Once the skin is crispy, turn it over and grill the other side for 3–4 minutes, until the chicken is cooked through. Remove from the heat and transfer the chicken to a chopping board. Leave to cool slightly then cut it into strips.

To assemble the salad, place some rice, quinoa or pearl barley, and slaw, in a bowl or on a plate, put the sliced chicken next to it and drizzle everything generously with the dressing. Sprinkle with coriander and mint and serve with a wedge of lime.

TIP: You can use chicken breast, but thigh meat is juicier. You can also cook this on the barbecue.

KERABU MEEHOON PEDAS DENGAN BEBOLA DAGING SERAI DAN HALIA

LEMONGRASS AND GINGER MEATBALLS WITH SPICY RICE VERMICELLI SALAD

Serves 4

For the meatballs
(makes 10 meatball 'lollipops',
    or 20 smaller meatballs)
200g minced pork
200g minced beef
2 tbsp fish sauce
1 tbsp light soy sauce
1 tsp caster sugar
20g ginger, peeled and finely diced
2 lemongrass stalks (tender base
    only), finely chopped
1 tbsp cornflour
1 tbsp vegetable oil

For the rice vermicelli salad
100g dried rice vermicelli
100g bean sprouts
juice of 1 lime
½ cucumber, sliced or julienned
10 baby plum tomatoes or cherry
    tomatoes, halved
4 coriander sprigs, leaves roughly
    torn
crispy shallots (optional, but so
    good)
1 × quantity Sambal Belacan
    (page 34)

I love meatballs, and mince is just the most versatile ingredient. Packed full of flavour, you can eat the meatballs on their own or serve them with this vermicelli salad. They also freeze well so you can double the recipe below and pop a batch in your freezer.

Soak 10 wooden skewers in water overnight, if using.

Mix the minced pork and beef together in a large bowl, then add all the remaining meatball ingredients, except the oil, cover and leave to marinate in the fridge for 2 hours.

Preheat the oven to 180°C/160°C fan/350°F/Gas 4. Take a little of the meatball mixture and, using the palm of your hand, shape it around a skewer. Alternatively, roll a little of the mixture between the palms of your hands and shape into balls.

Heat the vegetable oil in a frying pan and fry the meatballs for 1 minute on each side, then transfer them to an ovenproof dish (if the frying pan isn't suitable for the oven) and bake for 10 minutes.

Place the rice vermicelli and bean sprouts in a heat-proof bowl, cover with boiling water and leave to soak for 5 minutes, then drain and rinse under cold running water. Cut the vermicelli with scissors into short lengths.

In a large mixing bowl, combine all the ingredients for the salad together, except the crispy shallots, with enough Sambal Belacan to coat. Loosen with extra lime juice if the salad is too dry or spicy.

Divide the noodle salad between 4 bowls or plates, and place the meatballs on top. Sprinkle with crispy shallots, if using.

TIP: You can freeze the raw meatballs for another time. Defrost thoroughly before cooking.

KERABU MEEHOON NYONYA
SPICY PRAWN AND VERMICELLI SALAD

Serves 4

100g dry rice vermicelli (thin rice
  noodles or meehoon)
100g bean sprouts
30g unsweetened desiccated
  coconut
150g cooked king prawns
10 cherry tomatoes, halved
4 fresh Kaffir lime leaves, finely
  shredded
4 coriander sprigs, leaves chopped
3 small, round shallots, sliced
juice of ½ lime
1½ tbsp crispy shallots
½ tsp salt

For the dressing
1 quantity Sambal Belacan
  (page 34)
1½ tsp torch ginger bud purée
  (optional)

This Nyonya dish, which combines Malay and Chinese flavours, is superb. It predominantly consists of noodles and prawns, with a flourish of fresh herbs, cucumber to add crunch, and tomatoes to temper the fiery sambal dressing – all held together by toasted coconut to add fragrance.

Place the rice vermicelli and bean sprouts in a heat-proof bowl, cover with boiling water, and leave to soak for 5 minutes, then drain and rinse under cold running water.

Toast the desiccated coconut in a small frying pan, moving it around the pan with a spatula so it toasts evenly, until brown all over. Watch it like a hawk as it can burn very quickly. Remove from the heat, set aside and leave to cool.

Blend the sambal belacan with the torch ginger bud purée, if using.

In a large mixing bowl, combine all the ingredients, adding enough dressing and lime juice to coat it. Serve cold.

GADO-GADO

MALAYSIAN WARM SALAD OF VEGETABLES AND EGGS WITH SPICY PEANUT SAUCE

Serves 4

1 tbsp salt
20 green beans, topped and tailed
1 large carrot, peeled and cut into
   0.5cm rounds
1 large baking potato, peeled and
   cut into even small chunks
3 tbsp vegetable oil
½ a 200g block of tofu, cut into
   2cm cubes
½ cucumber, halved lengthways
   (unpeeled) and cut into 1cm
   half moons
100g bean sprouts

For the garnishes

2 medium free-range eggs
1 quantity Peanut Sauce (page 40)
8–10 ready-made prawn crackers
4 tbsp crispy shallots

This is a salad like no other. It sounds ordinary, but it holds a myriad of surprise textures and flavours. You can use pretty much any vegetables, but texture is important as every mouthful gives a different kind of crunch. The salad can be made in advance and then it is simply an assembly job. I tend to put different bowls of vegetables, garnishes and a large bowl of peanut sauce on the table and ask friends and family to help themselves.

Bring a saucepan of water to the boil and add the salt. Fill a large bowl with ice-cold water.

Add the green beans to the boiling water and bring it back up to the boil. Simmer for 2–3 minutes until they're cooked but still crunchy. Remove with a slotted spoon and drop them into the ice-cold water.

Add the carrot rounds to the boiling water and cook for 4 minutes, removing them with a slotted spoon and dropping them into the ice-cold water with the beans. Do the same with the potato chunks, cooking them for 10–15 minutes, until they're cooked through but not falling apart.

Heat the vegetable oil in a frying pan and fry the tofu for 15 minutes until brown. Remove and drain on kitchen paper.

Boil the eggs for 6 minutes if you want them soft-boiled, or 8 minutes if you prefer them hard-boiled. Once cool, peel away the shell and quarter the eggs.

Put the peanut sauce in a saucepan over a low heat and warm it through (do not let it boil).

Mix together the cooked vegetables, tofu, cucumber and bean sprouts, and divide among 4 bowls.

Place the peanut sauce and bowls of garnishes in the middle of the table. Spoon on a generous amount of peanut sauce over the vegetables, scatter with crumbled prawn crackers, crispy shallots and the eggs. Mix well and tuck in.

TIP: The other half-block of tofu can be used to make Mee Goreng Mamak (page 121).

SALAD SISA AYAM
LEFTOVER CHICKEN 'CLEAR YOUR FRIDGE' SALAD

Serves 2

100g dried rice vermicelli (optional)
150g leftover cooked chicken (or
    however much you have), torn
    into pieces
1 carrot, peeled and grated
handful of spinach leaves (or pretty
    much any salad leaves)
¼ cucumber, halved lengthways
    and cut into 0.5cm half moons
5–8 cherry tomatoes, halved
2–3 heaped tbsp Sambal Kampung
    (page 34)
1 tbsp crispy shallots, to serve

More often than not I have those bothersome little bits left in my fridge that haven't made it into a dish. The vegetable compartment is often littered with a few salad leaves, and perhaps half a carrot, but I can't bear to throw away food! Combine those leftovers, mix with Sambal Kampung and Bob's your uncle! I've used leftover roast chicken here, but pork or beef work well too.

Place the rice vermicelli, if using, in a heat-proof bowl, cover with boiling water, and leave to soak for 5 minutes, then drain and rinse under cold running water.

Combine the chicken, vegetables, tomatoes, rice vermicelli, if using, and the Sambal Kampung in a large mixing bowl then divide between 2 bowls. Sprinkle with crispy shallots to serve.

SUP AYAM MUDAH
SIMPLE CHICKEN BROTH

Serves 4

2 raw chicken carcasses
1½ litres water
1 tsp whole black peppercorns
1 onion, quartered (unpeeled)
8g slice of fresh root ginger,
    unpeeled

Chicken broth is so versatile, as you can enjoy it on its own, use it as a base for soups or to flavour stir-fries. I often buy a whole chicken, portion it up and freeze it for future use, and keep the carcass to make broth. Using a roast chicken carcass makes for a more intense broth; using raw bones makes a lighter broth.

Place the chicken carcasses in a saucepan, pour boiling water over them and bring the water back up to the boil. Boil over a high heat for 5 minutes then pour off the water. This helps get rid of any impurities in the broth.

Pour 1½ litres of fresh water into the saucepan and bring it up to the boil. Turn down the heat and add the peppercorns, onion and ginger. Cover and simmer for 1½ hours.

Remove and discard the carcasses. Pass the broth through a fine-mesh sieve and leave to cool.

TIP: The broth will keep for 2 days in the fridge, or can be frozen for up to 2 months.

SUP BABI DAN IKAN BILIS
SIMPLE PORK AND ANCHOVY BROTH

Serves 4

1kg pork bones
4 litres water
1 tsp vegetable oil
50g dried anchovies

My mum makes the most delicious broths. We call it broth as it is usually clear and thin, unlike the thick gloopy soups we have in Europe. My mum only uses the best ingredients for her broths, which she cooks slowly over charcoal for 4–6 hours so that all the nutrients and flavours are released. There are hundreds of broth recipes out there, but this one is the most versatile. The anchovies really add umami to the soup and mean you don't need to add seasoning. My mum believes broth should be eaten fresh and not stored but, if I can't finish it, I keep it in the fridge for one day, or freeze it for up to two months.

Place the bones in a saucepan large enough to fit them comfortably. Pour over half the water and bring to the boil. Boil for 10 minutes then pour off and discard all the water. This will get rid of all the impurities and ensure that your finished broth has a clearer and cleaner taste.

Pour the remaining 2 litres of water over the bones and bring to the boil.

Meanwhile, heat the oil in a frying pan and fry the dried anchovies for 1–2 minutes until they're crispy and golden brown. Add them to the saucepan. Cover and simmer the broth for 1½ hours, then pass it through a fine-mesh sieve.

You should have a flavoursome broth, which is delicious as it is, but also makes a good base for Porky Noodles (page 116) or Congee (page 108).

SUP ABC
ABC SOUP

Serves 4

1 raw or roast chicken carcass
1 medium carrot, cut into small
    chunks
3 medium onions, sliced
½ tsp black peppercorns
1 litre water
½ baking potato, peeled and cut
    into small chunks
3 tomatoes, quartered
salt, to taste
Garlic Oil (page 38), to serve
    (optional)

My mum always makes this soup for our family at home, though none of us can quite remember why it's called ABC! Using a chicken carcass makes it cheap and easy; in fact, it was the first soup I made when I moved to the UK. You can make it with the carcass of either a raw or roast chicken. The latter imparts a richer flavour, but may need more seasoning.

Place the chicken carcass (if using a raw one) in a saucepan, pour boiling water over it and bring the water back up to the boil. Boil over a high heat for 5 minutes then pour off the water. This helps get rid of any impurities in the broth. (If you are using the carcass of a roast chicken, omit this step.)

Place the carrot, onions and peppercorns in the same saucepan with the carcass.

Add the water to the pan, bring to the boil then simmer for 45 minutes. Add the potato and tomatoes. Bring to the boil again, then reduce the heat, cover and simmer for 30 minutes.

When the tomatoes and potato have softened, lift the carcass out of the pan, strip off any bits of meat and add them back to the soup (if you like). Discard the carcass. Add more water if the soup is too thick. I usually don't add salt to this broth, but feel free to add salt to taste. Fish out the whole peppercorns if you wish, before serving.

Finish the soup with a drizzle of Garlic Oil, if using, it's the bomb!

TIPS: You can bulk out this soup by adding cooked rice right at the end.

SUP AYAM DAN JAGUNG
CHICKEN AND SWEETCORN SOUP (non-gloopy version)

Serves 4

2 chicken thighs, bone in and
  skin on
1 tsp salt, plus extra to taste
½ quantity of Simple Chicken Broth
  (page 83)
198g tin of sweetcorn, drained well
Garlic Oil (page 38), to serve

The chicken and sweetcorn soup that I come across in this country tends to be thick and gloopy, worlds apart from the heart-warming kind I recall from my childhood. My mum used to make this soup on our charcoal hob, leaving it to slow-cook while she went to work so that it was ready when I came home from school. I would return home absolutely starving, creep into the kitchen and ladle the soup onto a bowl of steamed rice, finishing it off with a glug of garlic oil.

Rub the chicken thighs with the teaspoon of salt and set them aside for at least 20 minutes at room temperature.

Bring the broth to the boil in a saucepan and immerse the chicken thighs, then add the sweetcorn. Simmer for 30–40 minutes over a medium heat until the thighs are cooked through.

Lift the cooked thighs out of the broth. When they are cool enough to handle, strip the meat off the bones, and discard the bones and skin. Cut the meat into thin strips and add them back to the broth.

Season with salt to taste, drizzle with Garlic Oil and serve immediately.

TIP: You can ladle the soup over some fragrant steamed rice, drizzling it with Garlic Oil (page 38), to make it more of a substantial meal.

BAK WAN KEPITING
PORK AND CRABMEAT BROTH

Serves 4

150g fatty minced pork
65g crabmeat, tinned or fresh
2 tsp cornflour
2 spring onions, finely chopped
2 tsp chicken stock powder
¼ tsp ground white pepper
1.5 litres Simple Chicken Broth
    (page 83) or 2 tbsp chicken stock
    powder dissolved in 1.5 litres hot
    water
200g tin of bamboo shoots, drained
    and finely sliced
3 sprigs of coriander (leaves and
    stalks), chopped
2 tbsp crispy shallots, to serve
toasted sesame oil, for drizzling

Pork and crab is a classic combination in Chinese cookery, being the Asian version of surf and turf. This is a substantial broth that is seriously delicious.

Mix the minced pork, crabmeat, cornflour, spring onions, half the chicken stock powder and half the white pepper in a bowl. Leave to marinate for 10 minutes at room temperature.

Divide the crab and pork mixture into 12 balls then set aside.

Put the broth or stock in a saucepan and bring it to the boil. Add the remaining chicken stock powder, sliced bamboo shoots and remaining white pepper.

Gently drop the balls into the stock and simmer for 5–6 minutes over a medium heat until they float to the top.

Divide the balls between 4 bowls and pour the hot broth on top. Garnish with coriander and crispy shallots and a light drizzle of sesame oil.

TIP: You can substitute shelled king prawns for the crab, if you like, but blitz them in a blender first so they stick to the pork better.

SUP WONTON
QUICK WONTON SOUP

Makes 17–20 wontons (serves 2)

200g pack wonton skins (amount of
   skins wary)
1 litre Simple Chicken Broth
   (page 83) or 1½ tbsp chicken
   stock powder dissolved in 1 litre
   hot water
¼ tsp toasted sesame oil
1 spring onion, finely sliced

For the wontons
200g pork mince (not lean)
1 tbsp light soy sauce
¼ tsp salt
¼ tsp toasted sesame oil
½ tsp caster sugar
1 tbsp cornflour
large pinch of ground white pepper

Wontons are one of my favourite things to eat. I love them so
much that I served them in the MasterChef Final. To make this
soup more filling, serve with noodles.

To make the wontons, mix the pork mince in a bowl with the
remaining wonton ingredients and leave to marinate for at least
30 minutes at room temperature, or cover and leave to marinate
in the fridge overnight.

If you are using frozen wonton skins, then defrost them
thoroughly before using.

To make the wontons, place a skin on the palm of your hand
and arrange it in a diamond shape. Using a small teaspoon,
scoop a little of the marinated pork filling onto the middle of
the skin (don't be too greedy!). Dab 4 corners of the skin with
water and close your palm with enough pressure to seal the
wonton together. Make sure they are sealed properly by
pinching the top of the folds, ensuring there is no trapped air.

Repeat until you have used up all the filling. You will have
more than enough wontons for 2 people, and you can freeze
whatever you don't need for another meal.

Heat a saucepan of water on 1 burner of the hob, and heat
the broth or stock in another pan on another burner. Blanch
the wontons for 3 minutes in the water, then remove them with
a slotted spoon and transfer them to the broth to cook for a
further 3 minutes. You can do this in batches if you need to.
The blanching removes excess starch from the wonton skins.

Transfer the cooked wontons into bowls with some of the broth.
Drizzle with sesame oil and sprinkle with sliced spring onion.

TIPS: Pickled Green Chillies (page 41) go really well with
this soup.

If you have any excess skins, you can cut them into strips,
deep-fry them and sprinkle them over the soup.

RICE AND NOODLES

Rice and noodles are staples in Malaysian cuisine and we eat them at all times of day. My all-time favourite dish is Porky Noodles (page 116) from a stall outside my home in Ipoh, which I enjoy for breakfast. I also love rice, and it is the sole reason I got fat as a teenager. I have rice withdrawal symptoms if I go without it for more than four days.

Cultural associations with rice and noodle dishes abound. For example, we serve noodle dishes at the end of a celebratory birthday meal to indicate longevity. My aunty once told me: when you eat rice, be sure to finish every grain to ensure you don't end up with a spotty husband. Well, I adhered to that rule and I have to say I've hardly seen a spot on Andrew's face in the 16 years we've been together! Why risk it now?

I could write a whole book featuring just noodles and rice but until I do, these are my favourites and the ones I cook most often at home.

NASI PANDAN
PANDAN STEAMED RICE

Serves 4–6

300g jasmine rice
2 fresh pandan leaves, knotted
pinch of salt
thick slice of ginger

Pandan, also known as screw pine, is a fragrant leaf often used in desserts. It is, however, equally delicious when used to flavour rice. The rice takes on the subtle flavour of the pandan and goes very well with curries.

Wash the rice in cold water and drain, then repeat with fresh cold water. This will get rid of excess starch.

Place the rice in a saucepan or rice cooker. Fill the pan or rice cooker with cold water until it's 1cm above the rice.

Nestle the pandan leaves inside the rice and add the salt and ginger. If you are using a rice cooker at this point, turn it on and have a cup of tea! If you are using a saucepan, put it on the hob and bring it to the boil, then turn down the heat and simmer. As soon as the liquid is absorbed by the rice and bubbles start to form on the surface, turn off the heat, cover and let it steam for 30 minutes. Serve with your favourite curry.

NASI KUNYIT
TURMERIC RICE

Serves 4–6

1 tbsp vegetable oil
1 tsp black mustard seeds
1 tsp ground turmeric
6 fresh curry leaves (optional)
325g jasmine rice, rinsed twice
    and drained
1 tsp chicken stock powder
525ml water

This is a lighter version of the turmeric rice usually cooked in Malaysia, which is made with glutinous rice or 'sticky rice' as it's known here. It is a great accompaniment to any curry, and the striking yellow colour makes it really attractive.

Heat the oil in a heavy-based saucepan with a lid. Add the mustard seeds, and once the seeds start popping, add the turmeric, curry leaves, if using, and the rice. Stir to combine.

Add the chicken stock powder and water. Bring to the boil then turn the heat down and simmer. As soon as the liquid is absorbed by the rice and bubbles start to form on the surface, turn off the heat, cover and let it steam for 30 minutes. Remove the lid and use a fork to fluff up the rice before serving.

NASI GORENG AYAM DAN HALIA

GINGER AND CHICKEN FRIED RICE

Serves 4

200g jasmine rice, rinsed twice and
   drained (or 400g cooked leftover
   rice)
2 skinless, boneless chicken thighs,
   cut into 1cm cubes
1 tsp light soy sauce, to marinate
   the chicken
1 tbsp vegetable oil
2 garlic cloves, finely chopped
40g of fresh root ginger, cut into
   fine matchsticks
2 medium free-range eggs,
   lightly beaten
2 tsp light soy sauce
¼ tsp caster sugar

I love making this as it is so simple. My mum packed a little box of this rice for me when I was in primary school. I still recall eating it in the school playground and remember the smell and taste to this day. This is also a dish that mothers cook their daughters during their month-long confinement after giving birth. The Chinese believe that ginger helps expel built-up wind, restore the chi and helps the body recuperate faster. Just more reasons why I love it.

Cook the rice according to the packet instructions (it's best cooked the day before you make the fried rice), fluffing it up with a fork then setting it aside to cool. Alternatively, use leftover rice.

Place the cubed chicken in a bowl, add the soy sauce, mix together, then set aside for at least 20 minutes.

Heat the oil in a wok, add the garlic and ginger and fry for about 1 minute, until the ginger has softened. Add the chicken and fry until the chicken turns opaque, then push the chicken to the side of the wok furthest away from you, leaving a space at the front of the wok for the eggs. Pour the eggs into the wok and fry, stirring, until scrambled, then fold in the chicken. Stir-fry until the eggs begin to solidify.

Add the rice, light soy sauce and sugar to the wok and incorporate well, making sure there are no clumps of rice. Fry for a further 2 minutes, then remove from the heat and enjoy hot or at room temperature.

TIP: This keeps well for up to 2 days in the fridge, covered or stored in an airtight container. Reheat thoroughly – until piping hot – before serving.

NYONYA SOY-BRAISED WHOLE CHICKEN
WITH GARLIC BUTTER RICE

Serves 4–6

1 whole chicken (1–1.3kg)

1 tsp salt

1 tsp vegetable oil

30g galangal, skin on and cut into thick slices then bashed

20g fresh root ginger, skin on and cut into thick slices then bashed

3 spring onions, halved widthways

1 tsp black peppercorns

100ml dark soy sauce

50ml light soy sauce

4 tsp caster sugar, plus 1 tbsp for finishing the sauce

1.5 litres water, plus 3 tbsp

1 tbsp cornflour

slices of cucumber, to serve (optional)

Red Chilli and Ginger Dip (page 41), to serve (optional)

For the garlic butter rice

60g butter or margarine

400g jasmine rice, rinsed twice and drained

750ml chicken stock

2 garlic cloves, finely chopped

In Malaysia, most people don't have ovens to roast a chicken so they braise or steam it instead. This is a braised dish, in which the chicken simmers in a rich stock, and it is commonly eaten with rice. I find chicken cooked this way is more flavoursome than roasted chicken, and another bonus is that you can use the braising liquid as gravy.

Rub the chicken inside the cavity and over the skin with the salt and set aside for 20 minutes. Heat the oil in a wok or a large casserole dish and add the bashed galangal, ginger, spring onions and peppercorns. Fry for about 1 minute, until fragrant.

Add both soy sauces, the sugar and 1.5 litres of water to the wok or casserole dish and bring to the boil. Place the chicken in the liquid. Bring back to the boil, cover and simmer over a low heat for 40 minutes, turning the chicken a few times to ensure it is evenly cooked. If you don't have a lid for the wok, make a makeshift lid with foil and cover the top of the wok.

After 40 minutes, check if the chicken is cooked through: pierce the fattest part of the thigh with a skewer. The juices should run clear. If they don't, cook the chicken for a further 5–10 minutes, checking at 5-minute intervals.

Transfer the chicken carefully onto a serving plate and cover with foil to rest. Increase the heat under the wok or casserole dish and reduce the sauce for 20–30 minutes. Add the remaining sugar. Mix the cornflour with 3 tablespoons of water and add it to the sauce. Bring the sauce to the boil and adjust the seasoning if necessary.

While the sauce is reducing, cook the rice. Melt the butter in a saucepan, add the rice and stir to coat it in the butter. Pour in the chicken stock and simmer over a low heat. When the rice has absorbed nearly all the stock, add the garlic and mix it well into the rice, cover, remove from the heat and let it stand for at least 30 minutes. Remove the lid and fluff up the rice with a fork before serving.

Carve the chicken into big chunks. Place the pieces in a shallow serving tray and pour half of the sauce over the chicken and pour the rest into a jug. Serve with Garlic Butter Rice, extra sauce, slices of cucumber and Red Chilli and Ginger Dip.

STEAMED MINCED PORK RICE

Serves 2

150g minced pork (not lean)
130g jasmine rice
160ml water
2 tbsp kecap manis (sweet soy
    sauce)

For the marinade
½ tbsp oyster sauce
drizzle of toasted sesame oil
10g of fresh root ginger, peeled
    and finely diced
½ tsp cornflour
¼ tsp caster sugar

Minced pork is versatile, tasty and good value. I always have some marinated minced pork in the fridge or freezer, ready to be added to noodles or rice. This is a particularly good dish to make when you have that rare bit of time to yourself – curl up on the sofa with a glass or two of something and enjoy this warming bowl of rice – lucky you!

Place the minced pork in a bowl, add the marinade ingredients, stir to combine, cover and leave to marinate for at least 30 minutes, ideally overnight.

Get 2 saucepans and 2 heat-proof rice bowls ready, making sure the bowls fit comfortably into the saucepans (and that the saucepans can still be covered by the lids once the bowls are inside), and that you can lift the bowls out easily.

Divide the rice evenly between the 2 bowls. Rinse the rice in the bowls twice (with fresh cold water each time), to get rid of excess starch. Divide the water between the 2 bowls of rice and place them in the saucepans.

Carefully pour boiling water into the saucepans until the water is halfway up the bowls. Cover the pans and leave to steam over a medium–high heat for 10 minutes.

Divide the marinated minced pork into 2 patties and place a patty on top of each bowl of rice. Cover and steam for another 10 minutes. Drizzle 1 tablespoon of kecap manis over each bowl and steam for a further 5 minutes.

Carefully lift the bowls out of the saucepans and dig in.

TIP: Try serving this with Egg Foo Yung with Choi Sum and Onions (page 195) and a dollop of Shrimp Chilli Oil (page 43).

NASI AYAM CLAYPOT
CLAY POT CHICKEN RICE

Serves 2

3 dried shiitake mushrooms
150g boneless chicken thighs,
   sliced
1 tbsp vegetable oil
10g fresh root ginger, peeled and
   finely chopped
2 garlic cloves, finely chopped
1 Chinese sausage (lap cheong),
   sliced
4 tbsp sweet soy sauce
1 tbsp light soy sauce
3 tbsp water
200g jasmine rice
steamed bok choi, to serve
   (optional)
Bird's-eye Chilli and Soy Dip
   (page 39) and Stir-fried Lettuce
   (page 190), to serve (optional)

For the marinade
½ tsp light soy sauce
large pinch of caster sugar
½ tbsp cornflour

It is mesmerising to watch how street vendors make this dish as it takes multi-tasking to a whole new level. They have 10–12 charcoal stoves on the go at the same time, placing the clay pots with rice on top of the hob as the orders come in. As the rice and chicken are cooked, the rice forms an almost burnt crust, which gives the dish smokiness. The clay pot will need to be soaked if you're using it for the first time (pages 28–29). Alternatively, you can use a lidded casserole dish.

Put the dried shiitake mushrooms in a bowl, cover with cold water and set aside to rehydrate for 2 hours. You can speed up the rehydration by covering them with just-boiled water, if you prefer. Drain the mushrooms, squeeze them to discard excess water and cut off and discard the stalks. Quarter the mushrooms and set them aside.

Meanwhile, put the chicken in a bowl and add the marinade ingredients. Stir and leave to marinate for at least 20 minutes at room temperature, or 2 hours (covered) in the fridge.

Heat the oil in a frying pan, add the ginger and garlic and fry until fragrant, then add the sliced sausage and fry for a further minute. Add the marinated chicken and the mushrooms to the pan and continue to fry until the chicken turns opaque. Add half the sweet soy sauce and all the water. Continue to fry for a further 2 minutes (the chicken needs to be nearly cooked through). Set aside.

Wash the rice in cold water and drain, then repeat twice with fresh cold water. This will get rid of excess starch.

Transfer the drained rice to the clay pot, then fill it with water, until the water sits about 2.5cm above the rice. Bring it to the boil over a medium heat then turn the heat down to a low simmer.

After about 10 minutes, once the rice has absorbed nearly all the water, put the chicken mixture on top of the rice and cover the clay pot. Continue to cook on the hob over a low heat for a further 10–13 minutes. The rice will form a crust at the bottom of the pot. Serve with Bird's-eye Chilli and Soy Dip and the lettuce on the side.

NASI GORENG NYONYA

NYONYA FRIED RICE

Serves 4

200g jasmine rice, rinsed twice and
    drained (or 400g cooked leftover
    rice)
4 dried shiitake mushrooms
25g dried shrimps
3 tsp vegetable oil
2 free-range eggs, lightly beaten
2 shallots or ½ onion, thinly sliced
2 garlic cloves, finely chopped
150g raw peeled king prawns
1 tbsp oyster sauce
1 tsp light soy sauce
1 tsp dark soy sauce
large pinch of ground white pepper
3 tbsp crispy shallots, to serve
1 spring onion, finely sliced
1 red chilli, finely sliced, to serve
Shrimp Chilli Oil (page 43), to serve

This recipe is a one-pot wonder and a great store cupboard and freezer fallback.

Cook the rice according to the packet instructions (it's best cooked the day before you make the fried rice), fluffing it up with a fork then setting it aside to cool. Alternatively, use leftover rice.

Put the dried shiitake mushrooms in a bowl, cover with cold water and set aside to rehydrate for 2 hours. You can speed up the rehydration by covering them with just-boiled water (for 30–40 minutes) if you prefer. Drain the mushrooms, then chop them into rough dice (discarding the stalks) and set aside.

While the mushrooms are rehydrating, put the dried shrimps in a bowl, cover with cold water and set aside for 10 minutes. Drain and finely dice, then set aside.

Heat 1 teaspoon of the oil in a wok, pour in the beaten eggs and swirl the pan to make a thin omelette. As soon as the eggs cook through, roll up the omelette and transfer it to a plate. Once cool enough to handle, cut the omelette into thin slices.

Heat the remaining oil in the same wok over a medium heat, add the shallots and garlic and fry for 1½ minutes until fragrant. Add the dried shrimps and fry until aromatic and popping. Add the prawns and shiitake mushrooms and stir-fry until the prawns begin to turn pink. Add the cooked rice and mix it in thoroughly, making sure there are no clumps. Add the oyster sauce, soy sauces and white pepper and mix well, making sure that all the rice is well incorporated and that the prawns are cooked through. Add the omelette slices and remove from the heat.

Serve with crispy shallots, spring onion and sliced red chilli, and a big drizzle of Shrimp Chilli Oil.

TIP: Use a spatula when frying the eggs and rice as it's very useful for scraping all the bits from the surface of the wok.

NASI LEMAK
MALAYSIAN SPICY COCONUT RICE

Serves 4

For the coconut rice
300g jasmine or basmati rice
250ml coconut milk
200ml water
1 fresh pandan leaf, knotted
1cm thick slice of fresh root ginger,
   unpeeled
large pinch of salt

3 tbsp vegetable oil
8 tbsp Sambal Ikan Bilis (page 35)
4 free-range eggs
salted peanuts
½ cucumber, halved lengthways
   and cut into half moons
50g dried anchovies

This is my favourite rice meal of all time. It is a humble dish with humble ingredients, but combined they become far more than the sum of their parts. I can eat it day or night and my mum often buys it for breakfast from a stall near our house. You often find it presented in little banana leaf triangles at Mamak stalls or by street vendors in Malaysia. You can serve it with various accompaniments, such as Captain's Chicken Curry (page 151) or Beef Rendang (page 157), but I just like it as it is.

Wash the rice in cold water and drain, then repeat with fresh cold water. This will get rid of excess starch.

Place the rice in a saucepan or rice cooker and add the coconut milk and water. Nestle the pandan leaf in the rice with the ginger. Stir in the salt.

If using a rice cooker, put it on to cook and have a glass of wine. If you are using a saucepan, put it on the hob and bring to the boil, then reduce the heat and simmer. As soon as the liquid is absorbed by the rice and bubbles start to form on the surface, turn off the heat, cover and let it steam for 30 minutes.

Uncover the rice and fluff it up with a fork.

Heat the oil in a frying pan or wok, add the Sambal Ikan Bilis and fry for about 1 minute, until crispy and golden brown. Remove and drain on kitchen paper.

Fry the eggs in the same pan, according to your preference. I like mine with crispy edges, sunny side up. Alternatively, serve with soft boiled eggs.

Plate the rice with as much or as little sambal as you wish (I allow 2 tablespoons per person), a fried egg, peanuts, cucumber and crispy dried anchovies. To eat, just mix it all together and enjoy.

JUK
CONGEE

Serves 3–4

150g jasmine rice
1cm thick slice of fresh root ginger, unpeeled
750ml water or broth such as Simple Pork and Anchovy Broth (page 85) or Simple Chicken Broth (page 83)
1 century egg, at room temperature, to serve (optional)
1 salted egg to serve (optional)
182g can pickled lettuce, drained, to serve (optional)

In east Asia this is often called *juk*. It has a porridge-like consistency, though unlike porridge it is savoury. When I'm feeling a bit under the weather, I make congee, eating it plain, or with meat or fish – it is my ultimate comfort food and hangover cure. When I was weaning Alexa I'd make her a nutrient-packed salt-free version. My favourite congee of all time is the 'mixed pig' congee, or *chu chap juk* as it's called in Malaysia. Unfortunately, some of the 'piggy bits' you find in chu chap juk are hard to source here in the UK, but if you're in Malaysia, you must try it. Congee can be eaten on its own if made with broth, or served as an accompaniment to a meat or fish dish. I love mine with salted and century eggs, and a bit of pickled lettuce for crunch.

Wash the rice in cold water and drain, then repeat twice with fresh cold water. This will get rid of excess starch.

Put the rice in a saucepan with the ginger and water or broth and bring it to the boil.

Turn down the heat and simmer, uncovered, for 30–40 minutes, until the rice breaks down, stirring it often so that the rice doesn't stick to the bottom of the pan. If it gets too thick, add some water.

If you are serving your congee with a century egg, just peel away the shell and cut the egg into quarters. If you are serving it with a salted egg, boil the egg for 15–18 minutes. Lift out the egg from the water and leave until cool enough to handle, then cut the egg in half and scoop the egg out of the shell with a spoon.

CILI PAN MEE

CHILLI PAN MEE

Serves 4

For the handmade noodles
400g plain flour, plus extra for dusting
2 medium free-range eggs
½ tsp salt
150ml cold water

For the pork
250g minced pork (not lean)
6 dried shiitake mushrooms
2 tsp vegetable oil
2 garlic cloves, thinly sliced
1 tbsp oyster sauce
1 tsp sweet soy sauce
250ml water, plus 3 tbsp
1 tsp dark soy sauce
1 tsp cornflour

For the marinade
2 tsp cornflour
1 tbsp light soy sauce
½ tsp caster sugar
2 large pinches of ground white pepper

To garnish
3 tbsp vegetable oil, plus extra for dressing
20g dried anchovies
4 free-range eggs
4 spring onions, sliced
4 tbsp crispy shallots
4 tbsp Shrimp Chilli Oil (page 43)

Pan mee noodles are traditionally hand-pulled into different-sized pieces and served in an anchovy broth with sweet potato leaves and minced pork. In Malaysia it's commonly eaten for breakfast, but like most noodle dishes you can eat them at any time of day.

Place the minced pork in a bowl and add the marinade ingredients. Mix well and leave to marinate for at least 10 minutes at room temperature or covered, in the fridge, overnight.

Put the dried shiitake mushrooms in a bowl, cover with cold water and set aside to rehydrate for 2 hours. You can speed up the rehydration by covering them with just-boiled water, if you prefer. Drain, remove the stalks, cut into dice and set aside.

To make the noodle dough, combine the flour, eggs and salt in a bowl, then gradually add 150ml of cold water and mix until the dough comes together. Transfer the sticky dough to a lightly floured work surface and knead for 5–10 minutes until smooth. If it is too wet, add more flour when kneading. Wrap the dough in cling film and leave to rest for 30 minutes in the fridge.

Heat the oil for the pork in a frying pan, add the garlic and fry until fragrant, then add the rehydrated shiitake mushrooms. Fry for 2 minutes, then add the minced pork, breaking it down with a spoon to make sure there are no big clumps. Fry until the pork is no longer pink, then add the oyster sauce, sweet soy sauce, dark soy sauce and 200ml of water.

Simmer over a low heat for 5–10 minutes, until almost all the water has evaporated. Add the remaining 50ml of water, bring it to the boil, then dissolve the cornflour in 3 tablespoons of water and add it to the pan. Bring to the boil, stir, and once the sauce has thickened and is coating the pork, remove from the heat and set aside.

Heat 3 tablespoons of vegetable oil in a small frying pan. Fry the anchovies gently for 1–2 minutes until they are brown and crispy, then remove with a slotted spoon and transfer to kitchen paper. Set aside.

Recipe continues overleaf

Remove the noodle dough from the fridge, divide it into 4 pieces and flatten each piece with the palm of your hand. Dust them lightly with flour then, using a pasta machine, roll out the dough, starting with the 1st or thickest setting, progressing to the 4th. Cut each strip in half lengthways to make 8 strips. Fix the tagliatelle attachment to the machine and roll the dough through, 1 strip at a time. Transfer the noodles to a floured baking tray and toss them in the flour to prevent them sticking.

Bring a large pot of water to a rolling boil, add half or a third of the noodles and cook for 1 minute, until tender but still slightly al dente. If the water gets too starchy, add some fresh boiling water and bring it up to the boil before you cook the next batch. Drain the noodles and dress with a little vegetable oil.

Fill a separate, small deep saucepan with water and bring to a rolling boil. Crack an egg into a ramekin or a cup. Using a wooden spoon, swirl the water to create a whirlpool. Gently pour the egg into the middle of the swirling water. Poach for 3 minutes. Remove the egg using a slotted spoon. Repeat with remaining 3 eggs.

To assemble, divide the noodles between 4 bowls, top with the pork mixture and add a poached egg to each bowl, followed by the spring onions and crispy shallots, and a dollop of Shrimp Chilli Oil. Mix all the ingredients together thoroughly before eating.

TIP: The noodles are tricky to make by hand if you don't have a pasta machine, so if you don't have one at home, use shop-bought wheat noodles instead.

Don't worry about using plenty of flour to dust the noodles – the cooking process will get rid of the excess starch.

113

KARI LAKSA NYONYA
NYONYA CURRY LAKSA

Serves 4

1.2 litres water
1 quantity of Laksa Paste (page 33)
250ml coconut milk
1 tbsp chicken stock powder
1 tbsp of salt
6 pieces of bean curd puff,
  cut in half
100g dried rice vermicelli
50g bean sprouts
400g pack of fresh yellow noodles
salt (optional)

For the chicken and prawns
2 boneless chicken thighs, skin on
¼ tsp salt
350ml water
½ lemongrass stalk, bashed
200g shelled raw tiger prawns

For the garnish
bunch of mint leaves
2 medium free-range eggs, soft
  boiled or hard boiled, peeled
  and halved
4 lime wedges
4 tsp Shrimp Chilli Oil (page 43)
crispy shallots, to serve

This hot, steaming bowl of fragrant, spicy broth with noodles, prawns and egg is a common dish in Malaysia. The key component is the spice paste, which takes a bit of time, but once you've made it, you can keep it in the fridge for up to a month. Alternatively, there are very good shop-bought pastes available.

Rub the chicken thighs with salt and set aside for at least 20 minutes at room temperature.

Place the chicken in a saucepan, cover with the water and salt, add the lemongrass, bring to a simmer and poach over a low heat for 15–20 minutes. Remove the chicken and set aside to cool, then cut the meat into strips, discarding the skin. Poach the prawns for 2–3 minutes in the same poaching liquid. Once they are cooked, remove them with a slotted spoon and set aside. Instead of just using water, you can use the poaching liquid to make the laksa broth – just top it up with water until it reaches 1.2 litres and discard the lemongrass stalk.

Bring the water or poaching liquid, laksa paste, coconut milk, chicken stock powder and salt to the boil. Add the bean curd puff and simmer for 5 minutes, then remove from the heat, taste and add salt if necessary.

Place the rice vermicelli and bean sprouts in a heat-proof bowl, cover with boiling water and leave to soak for 5 minutes, then add the fresh yellow noodles to the hot water and leave them for 3 minutes. Drain the vermicelli, bean sprouts and noodles and divide them between 4 serving bowls.

Arrange slices of chicken, prawns, a few mint leaves and the halved eggs on top of noodles.

Strain the laksa broth through a fine sieve into a bowl or jug and remove the bean curd puffs. Place 3 slices of puff on top of each bowl of noodles. Make sure that the broth is still piping hot (heat it again if not), pour the broth over the noodles.

Serve with lime wedges, Shrimp Chilli Oil and a sprinkling of crispy shallots.

MINCED PORK WITH CORIANDER
AND FISH SAUCE NOODLES

Serves 4

500g minced pork (not lean)
1 tbsp vegetable oil
2 garlic cloves, finely chopped
2 tbsp fish sauce
2 tbsp sweet soy sauce
½ tsp caster sugar
250ml water, plus 2 tbsp
1½ tbsp cornflour
40g coriander, chopped (stalks
  and all)

For the marinade
1½ tbsp cornflour
1 tbsp oyster sauce
2 tbsp light soy sauce
½ tsp caster sugar
¼ tsp ground white pepper

For the noodles
4 x 100g bundles of egg or wonton
  noodles
2 tbsp Garlic Oil (page 38)
2 tbsp sweet soy sauce
2 tbsp oyster sauce

This is one of my favourite dishes that Mum would make me for school. I'd often wolf it down in the car en route, and go into school stinking of garlic, but I didn't care as it was so tasty. Now that I am a mum I often cook this for my daughter. A kind of Asian bolognaise, it is versatile, easy to make and keeps well in the fridge. I normally serve it with wonton or egg noodles.

Put the minced pork in a bowl, mix with the marinade ingredients and set aside for at least 15 minutes at room temperature, or longer if you prefer, covered in the fridge.

Heat the oil in a wok or frying pan over a medium heat. Add the garlic and fry until fragrant, then add the marinated pork and fry gently (a high heat will dry out the pork), breaking up the mince while it cooks, until it is no longer pink.

Add the fish sauce, sweet soy sauce and sugar, then add the 250ml of water. Bring to the water to the boil, then lower the heat and simmer gently for 5 minutes. If you think there's too much water, don't worry – soon it will thicken and be absorbed by the pork.

Dissolve the cornflour in 2 tablespoons of water and add it to the pork and bring to the boil. As it boils, the sauce will thicken and coat the pork. At this stage fold in the coriander and remove the wok or pan from the heat.

Cook the egg or wonton noodles for 2 minutes. Drain well and coat lightly with the garlic oil. Season with sweet soy sauce and oyster sauce. Top with a generous dollop of the pork mixture.

To eat, mix it together and slurp loudly!

TIPS: You can also use chicken thighs for this dish, if you prefer, chopped rather than minced.

Serve with egg noodles, flat rice noodles, rice or congee (page 108), instead of wonton noodles, if you like.

PRAWN CHA KEOW TEOW
STIR-FRIED FLAT RICE NOODLES WITH PRAWNS

Serves 4

200g flat rice noodles
2 tbsp vegetable oil, plus extra for
    drizzling
1 onion, thickly sliced
1 garlic clove, finely chopped
4–6 garlic chives, sliced into batons
200g raw shelled king prawns
2 free-range eggs, beaten
2 tbsp sweet soy sauce
2 tbsp light soy sauce
1 tbsp dark soy sauce (optional)
180g bean sprouts

This is a very popular dish in Malaysia and my family's favourite. The high heat the noodles are fried over means they take on a smoky flavour; rumour has it that the vendors don't wash their wok so the char from previous stir-fries adds to the smokiness. It is difficult to replicate the smokiness of this dish at home but the charring of the onions and noodles helps. In Malaysia we can choose which noodles we want as well as what goes in with them. Each member of my family has their own favourite combination. My dad's *cha keow teow* always has a mixture of flat rice and thin rice noodles with prawns, eggs and cockles.

Bring a saucepan of water to the boil and cook the noodles for about 10 minutes, or until soft but still with a bit of bite. Drain and drizzle with a little vegetable oil to stop them sticking.

Heat the oil in a wok or large frying pan over a high heat until smoking, then add the onion and stir them constantly. You want to char the onions but not burn them. Add the garlic and garlic chives. Stir for 1 minute, then add the cooked noodles. Let the mixture sit for a minute over the heat, untouched.

Add the prawns to the wok or pan and stir-fry for 1 minute. Push everything to the edge of the wok furthest away from you and add the beaten eggs to the empty part of the pan. Stir, to cook the eggs a little, then gently fold the rest of the ingredients into the eggs until well incorporated.

Add the sweet soy sauce, light soy sauce and dark soy sauce, if using, and stir-fry well for 30 seconds.

Finally, tip the bean sprouts into the wok and work them through the noodles. They cook very quickly and are ready when they have just softened. You want to keep their crunchiness. Taste and add more soy sauce or sweet soy sauce if necessary. Serve immediately.

MEE GORENG MAMAK
FRIED MAMAK NOODLES

Serves 4

3 tbsp vegetable oil
½ a 200g block firm tofu, cut into
   3cm cubes
2 garlic cloves, finely chopped
200g raw peeled tiger prawns
1 tomato, cut into 6 wedges
2 stalks of choi sum, roughly
   chopped
400g pack of fresh yellow noodles
2 spring onions, sliced
100g bean sprouts
salt, to taste
4 lime wedges, to serve
3 tbsp crispy shallots, to serve

For the chilli paste

3 fresh red chillies
1 tbsp water

For the sauce

1 tbsp sweet soy sauce
2 tbsp oyster sauce
3 tbsp tomato ketchup
1 tsp dark soy sauce
¼ tsp salt
1 tsp crispy prawn chillies (optional)

I love this noodle dish so much that when I'm in Malaysia I always go out of my way to find it, and often eat it for breakfast. It comes with a sticky sauce that is both spicy and sweet, and is served with half a calamansi (a fruit that tastes like a clementine crossed with a lime) on the side.

Mix all the ingredients for the sauce in a small bowl.

Put the chillies and water for the chilli paste in a small blender and blitz to form a paste.

Heat the oil in a wok or large frying pan and fry the cubed tofu for about 15 minutes, until browned all over. Remove and drain on kitchen paper.

Using the same wok, add the garlic and chilli paste and fry for 1 minute. Add the prawns and fry until they start to turn pink, then add the tomato and choi sum and stir-fry for a further minute. Add the noodles, browned tofu and sauce, then the spring onions and bean sprouts. Mix well and make sure the prawns are cooked through.

Check the seasoning and serve immediately, with lime wedges and crispy shallots. Squeeze over the juice from the lime before eating.

LAP CHEONG UDON
STIR-FRIED UDON WITH CHINESE SAUSAGE

Serves 2

1 tbsp vegetable oil
2 Chinese sausages (lap cheong),
   thinly sliced
1 small onion, sliced into half moons
2 garlic cloves, roughly chopped
200g pack of udon noodles
2 tbsp water
1 tbsp oyster sauce
2 tsp light soy sauce
1 tsp Shrimp Chilli Oil (page 43)
   or crispy prawn chillies (optional)
1 spring onion, finely chopped
1 tbsp crispy shallots

This is my husband Andrew's creation, really. If we eat our main meal during the day and just want a light dinner in the evening, he will make this noodle dish. It's a great pantry standby as it requires few fresh ingredients. You can also pretty much throw any leftover vegetables into it.

Heat the oil in a wok or frying pan and fry the sausage and onion for 2–3 minutes until the sausage is crispy and the onions have softened. Add the garlic and fry for a further 30 seconds, then add the udon noodles and water. Fry for about 30 seconds, then add the oyster and soy sauce. Fry for 1 minute, then add the Shrimp Chilli Oil or crispy prawn chillies, if using. Remove from the heat and sprinkle with chopped spring onion and crispy shallots.

CHU YUK FUN
PORKY NOODLES

Serves 2

125g minced pork (not lean)
1 quantity of Simple Pork and
   Anchovy Broth (page 85)
200g pork belly, skin on
200g pack of udon noodles
90g pork liver, trimmed and cut into
   very thin slices
1 tbsp Garlic Oil (page 38)
small handful of coriander, chopped
1 spring onion, finely chopped
salt, to taste
Bird's-eye Chilli and Soy Dip
   (page 39), to serve

For the marinade
½ tsp light soy sauce
½ tsp cornflour
pinch of caster sugar
pinch of salt
drizzle of toasted sesame oil

TIP: If you don't have time to make the broth from scratch, make an instant broth: bring 1.5 litres of water to the boil and add ½ tablespoon of chicken stock powder.

The broth is the king in this dish, so it is worth taking the time to make it from scratch, but if time isn't on your side, you can cheat (see TIP). My favourite noodles for this dish are *lo shu fan*, but they can be difficult to find in the UK so udon noodles, vermicelli or flat rice noodles are fine substitutes. Alternatively, you can use macaroni (page 202).

Place the minced pork in a bowl, add the marinade ingredients, mix well and leave to marinate for at least 10 minutes at room temperature (or covered, in the fridge, overnight).

Rub the flesh and skin of the pork belly with salt and set aside on a plate for at least 30 minutes, or in a sealed container overnight in the fridge, if you like.

When you are ready to cook the dish, remove the marinated minced pork from the fridge (if you were marinating it overnight) and let it come back to room temperature.

Bring the broth to the boil in a saucepan and drop in the pork belly. Let it cook for 15–20 minutes, and once it's cooked through, lift it out and set it aside, keeping the broth over the heat. Once cool, cut the pork into slices (discard the skin if you prefer).

Bring a separate pan of water to the boil, place the noodles in the pan and cook for 2 minutes, until the noodles soften. Drain and divide them between 2 bowls. Place the sliced pork belly on top and keep warm.

Take a teaspoon of marinated minced pork and shape it into a rough ball in the palm of your hand then drop it into the broth. Repeat until all the mixture is in the broth, and cook the balls for 3–4 minutes (they float to the top when cooked).

Keeping the broth at a rolling boil, add the thinly sliced liver, stir and immediately remove from the heat.

Lift the liver and pork balls out of the broth with a slotted spoon and divide between the 2 bowls, then ladle over the hot broth to cover the noodles.

Drizzle over the garlic oil and scatter with chopped coriander and spring onion. Serve with Bird's-eye Chilli and Soy Dip.

NGAU YUK FUN
BEEF NOODLES ACROSS TWO BORDERS

Makes 2 exquisite bowls

For the beef broth
1.5kg beef bones
5cm of cinnamon stick
30g fresh root ginger, cut into thick
　slices, unpeeled
2 star anise
8 cloves
1.7 litres water
1½ tbsp chicken stock powder
200g mooli or daikon (page 56),
　peeled and cut into small chunks
　(optional)
50g calves liver, trimmed, very thinly
　sliced and covered with cold water
　until required
100g prime beef fillet, very thinly
　sliced, at room temperature
few pinches of sea salt
2 x 100g balls of wonton noodles
vegetable oil, for dressing
1 spring onion, finely chopped
4–5 celery leaves (from the top of
　celery heads)
Bird's-eye Chilli and Soy Dip
　(page 39) or dried red chilli flakes,
　to serve

TIP: You can get beef bones from
your local butcher. Ask them to
chop the bones into smaller pieces
so you can fit them in your pan.

This is a wonderfully comforting dish inspired by both a
delicious food stall in my home town and one in Thailand.

Preheat the oven to 200°C/180°C fan/400°F/Gas 6. Place the
beef bones in a roasting tin and roast for 20 minutes.

Put the roasted beef bones, cinnamon, star anise, cloves,
water and chicken stock powder in a large saucepan and bring
them to the boil. Lower the heat and simmer for 1½ hours.
After 15 minutes of simmering, remove the cinnamon.

Add the mooli, if using, to the pan after the broth has been
simmering for 1½ hours, and simmer for a further 20–30
minutes, until softened. If you are not using the radishes, ignore
this step and just simmer the broth for 1¾ hours.

Strain the broth through a fine sieve into a separate pan and
set aside, discarding everything left in the sieve except the
mooli, if using, – place these in the broth.

Drain the calves liver and pat it dry. Season the beef fillet and
calves liver with a pinch of salt and set aside.

Bring the broth to the boil and season with salt to taste.

Bring a separate pan of water to the boil, add a pinch of salt
and cook the noodles for a couple of minutes until tender but
still slightly al dente. Drain in a colander. If the noodles are a
little slimy, keep them in the colander and pour over some
boiling water to get rid of the excess starch. Dress the noodles
with a little vegetable oil to keep them from sticking and divide
them between 2 bowls.

Arrange slices of beef fillet on top of the noodles.

Place all the slithers of calves liver in a large slotted spoon,
then lower them into the broth and cook for 10–15 seconds.
Lift them out and arrange them on top of noodles.

Fish the mooli, if using, out of the broth and place them
around the meat in the bowls. Make sure the broth is still boiling
and ladle it generously over the beef and liver and garnish
generously with spring onion and celery leaves.

Serve immediately with Chilli and Soy Dip or a large pinch of
dried red chilli flakes.

HOKKIEN MEE
CHEAT'S PRAWN NOODLES

Serves 2

6 large tiger prawns, with heads and
  shells on
3 tbsp prawn noodle paste
1 boneless, skinless chicken thigh
¼ tsp salt
25g bean sprouts
2 sprigs kangkung or Chinese water
  spinach, washed, drained and cut
  into 6cm slices
2 tsp vegetable oil
1 litre water
1 tbsp chicken stock powder
200g fresh yellow noodles
1 free-range egg, soft- or hard-
  boiled, peeled and halved
  (page 66)
Shrimp Chilli Oil (page 43), to serve
  (optional)

**What's the cheat element? Well it is possible to make this dish
from scratch, but given it would require 1kg of prawn shells, it
would be expensive. Sometimes it's worth taking a shortcut!**

Remove the heads and shells from 4 of the prawns, mix them
in ½ a tablespoon of the prawn noodle paste and set aside to
marinate. Place the 4 peeled prawns and the remaining 2 whole
prawns with another ½ tablespoon of the paste and set aside.

Put the chicken thigh and salt in a small saucepan and add
enough water to cover the chicken. Bring to the boil, turn down
the heat to low and simmer for 20–30 minutes until cooked.
Remove the chicken from the poaching liquid, set aside to cool
then slice thinly.

Add the bean sprouts to the same liquid with the kangkung
and poach for 30 seconds. Remove with a slotted spoon and
set aside. Retain the poaching liquid to add to the broth later.

Heat most of the oil in a frying pan and fry the marinated
prawn heads and shells over a medium–high heat for about
5 minutes. Crush them slightly with the back of a wooden
spoon while they're frying.

In a saucepan, bring the water, chicken stock powder and the
remaining prawn paste to the boil. Add a spoonful of this broth
to the fried prawn shells to deglaze the pan then tip all the shells
and poaching liquid back into the broth. Simmer for 15 minutes.

Heat the remaining oil (about 1 teaspoon) in the same frying
pan you used for the prawn shells and pan-fry the marinated
prawns for 3–4 minutes, until cooked. The whole ones might
take a little longer than the peeled ones.

Put the fresh yellow noodles in a heat-proof bowl, cover with
boiling water and leave to soak for 3 minutes, then drain. Divide
the noodles between 2 bowls. Arrange the sliced chicken,
shelled and unshelled prawns, bean sprouts, kangkung and
half an egg on top of the noodles.

Strain the broth through a fine sieve. Crush the shells with the
back of a wooden spoon to extract all the flavour. Discard the
shells. Ladle over enough soup to cover the noodles and prawns.
Serve with a drizzle of Shrimp Chilli Oil for extra kick.

ROTI JALA
MALAYSIAN NET PANCAKES

Makes about 8 pancakes

100g plain flour
⅓ tsp salt
⅓ tsp turmeric
1 free-range egg
100ml water
100ml semi-skimmed milk
vegetable oil, for frying

Malaysian net pancakes are a brilliant accompaniment to curries, as an alternative to rice. They resembles a net, hence the name, and they are soft and slightly chewy in texture. When dipped into curry, they hold the sauce really well. Traditionally, to create the net pattern, a special mould is used, but to get a similar effect you can just pour the batter into a squeezy bottle and swirl it into the pan, or just make a normal pancake without the pattern – it tastes just as good!

Mix the flour, salt and turmeric together. Beat the egg and add it to the flour mixture, then add the water and milk. Whisk the batter well to avoid lumps.

Strain the batter through a sieve and into a jug. Transfer the batter into a squeezy bottle, or cook as you would cook normal pancakes.

Heat a little oil in a non-stick frying pan over a medium heat (you only need enough to coat the pan) and drizzle the batter as quickly as you can into the pan, in a random fashion, to form a net (if you like). Cook for 30–40 seconds on 1 side, then flip the pancake to cook it on the other side. They cook really quickly so watch them closely. Repeat until you have used up all the batter, placing the cooked pancakes between layers of greaseproof paper to stop them sticking.

You can serve the pancakes flat or rolled up. To roll, fold the 2 sides in (about 1cm in on both sides), then roll up.

MEAT AND POULTRY

Sometimes, when I'm home in Malaysia, I'll go with my mum to the wet market in Ipoh. Our first stops are always to the pork man and then the chicken man and she's their best customer. My mother is a master at shopping and very pernickety when it comes to the quality of the produce. The traders are a little scared of her as they've received much of her wrath over the years when their stock wasn't at its best! I dedicate this section to my mum's butchers and to mine, Larkhall Butchers in Bath, as they work very hard to bring the best produce to our kitchen table.

   The dishes in this section have influences from Malay, Chinese and Indian cooking. They are usually eaten accompanied with other meat, fish or vegetable dishes but are substantial enough to enjoy on their own with plain rice or vegetables.

KARAMEL TAU EU BAK
CARAMEL PORK BELLY WITH SOY

Serves 4

3 pieces of dried wood ear
    mushrooms (optional)
2 tbsp caster sugar
2 thick slices of fresh root ginger,
    skin on
4 garlic cloves, lightly bashed
500g pork belly, skin on, cut into
    2cm cubes
1½ tbsp light soy sauce
1 tbsp dark soy sauce
500ml water

This is one of my mum's specialities. It's a heart-warming, rich, smoky dish that's best cooked the day before you eat it, to give the flavours a chance to develop. It is quick and simple to make too, and uses my favourite part of the pig: the belly. I leave the skin on the belly to keep the meat moist during braising, but you can always discard the skin before eating, or use skinless pork belly. Dried wood ear mushrooms are ideal for this dish – they don't add much flavour but they do add a welcome texture. Serve with fluffy rice or congee.

Place the pieces of wood ear mushrooms, if using, in a large bowl, cover with cold water, and leave to rehydrate for 2 hours. Drain and squeeze out the excess water then cut off and discard the hard parts and chop the soft mushrooms into 4cm pieces.

Sprinkle the sugar into a stainless steel saucepan, and place over a low–medium heat. Watch it like a hawk. As soon as the sugar melts and turns dark brown (don't let it burn), add the ginger and garlic and let them sear in the caramel for 30 seconds until fragrant.

Add the cubes of pork belly to the pan, turn up the heat slightly and stir to ensure the pork is coated in the caramel. Add both the soy sauces and the water, and the drained wood ear mushrooms, if using.

Bring to the boil then turn the heat down to low and simmer for 1½ hours. Remove from the heat. Once cool, spoon the excess fat off the top.

Chill in the fridge overnight, then reheat until piping hot and serve with fluffy white rice or congee.

TIP: This dish is rich, but the Thai Basil and Sweet Chilli Dip (page 38) will help cut through the fattiness of the pork and balance out the dish nicely.

SIU YUK

CANTONESE ROAST PORK

Serves 4

1kg pork belly, boneless with skin on
500ml water
100ml white vinegar
2 tbsp coarse sea salt
distilled white vinegar, for brushing
plain rice, to serve
Shrimp Chilli Oil (page 43), to serve
    (optional)

For the dry rub
2 tbsp coarse sea salt
1 tbsp whole Szechuan peppercorns
1 tsp whole black pepper
    peppercorns
2 tsp five-spice powder
2 tsp granulated sugar

If I was a pig, I would want to die and be cooked as Cantonese roast pork. I think it is the best way a piece of belly can be cooked and the Chinese are experts at it.

There aren't many ingredients, but it does take a bit of time to prepare. I promise you, it's worth it. Try to hold back some leftover meat to make the Stir-fried Chinese Roast Pork with Leeks (page 138).

Prick the pork skin all over with a small knife or a safety pin.

Mix the water and vinegar together in a wok or large frying pan and bring to the boil.

Using a carving fork or a meat hook (if you have one) pierce through the meat side, lift the pork over the wok and ladle the water and vinegar mixture all over the skin 5–10 times. Put the pork on a board or plate, pat dry with kitchen paper and set aside.

Put all the ingredients for the dry rub in a dry wok or frying pan and fry for 2–3 minutes, taking care not to burn the sugar. Transfer the mixture to a pestle and mortar and crush to a fine powder.

Rub 2 tablespoons of the mixture onto the meat side of the pork. Place the belly meat-side down on a tray. Rub the skin with half of the coarse sea salt. Leave uncovered and place in the fridge. After 1 hour, take the pork out, remove the salt and pat the skin dry. Put the pork back in the fridge, uncovered, and leave it overnight.

The next day, remove the pork from the fridge and rub the remaining coarse sea salt on the skin and leave it at room temperature for 1 hour. Preheat the oven to 200°C/180°C fan/400°F/Gas 6. Remove the salt from the pork skin and pat it dry with kitchen paper again.

Place the pork belly skin-side up on a wire rack, and place the rack over a roasting tin (it should sit over the tin, not inside it). Fill the tin halfway with water (the water shouldn't touch the pork).

Place the pork in the oven and roast for 20 minutes.

Remove the pork from the oven, pat the skin dry with kitchen paper and brush it with some vinegar.

Turn the oven down to 150°C/130°C fan/300°F/Gas 2, return the pork to the oven and cook for a further 30 minutes.

Remove the pork from the oven, pat the skin dry with kitchen paper and brush the skin again with vinegar. Return the pork to the oven and cook for a further 30 minutes.

If the skin has not crisped up, place it under the grill under a medium heat. Slice the meat into chunks and serve with rice and Shrimp Chilli Oil, if using.

PAU CHU YUK

STIR-FRIED CHINESE ROAST PORK WITH LEEKS

Serves 4

1 tbsp vegetable oil
300g leftover Roast Cantonese Pork
  (page 134) or shop-bought roast
  pork from a Chinese supermarket,
  cut into 3cm cubes
2 garlic cloves, roughly chopped
1 tsp light soy sauce
3 tsp sweet soy sauce
400g leeks, cut into thick strips
  lengthways, washed thoroughly
  and drained
5 tbsp water
¼ tsp caster sugar
1 tsp dark soy sauce

There is a restaurant in Ipoh called Kafe Yoon Wah in Jalan Bijih Timah, in the old part of the city, which my brother took me to during my first visit back to Malaysia with my in-laws. My parents and Andrew's had never met, despite us being together for nine years at that point. The food in this casual restaurant is incredible, as are the drinks which are the house speciality. They serve 'snow beer' in frozen mugs, which is poured in quickly to form tiny crystals – a 'beer smoothie', if you like, which is heaven in a country as hot as Malaysia. All the food they serve revolves around what works well with the beer, and this dish is the most memorable one for me. They use Chinese leeks which are very pungent but I use regular leeks and pair them with my Cantonese roast pork – it's seriously delicious. I thoroughly recommend enjoying it with an ice-cold beer!

Heat the oil in a wok or large non-stick frying pan over a high heat until smoking, then add the pork and fry for 1 minute, turning the heat down to medium if it is too smoky. Add the garlic and stir-fry for another minute.

Add the light soy sauce to the fried pork and garlic and toss to coat the pork. Cook for 1 minute until the soy sauce has almost evaporated.

Add the sweet soy sauce and leeks with 2 tablespoons of the water. Stir-fry for about 4 minutes, until the leeks have started to soften, then add the sugar, dark soy sauce and the remaining water. Stir-fry until the leeks have completely softened and have a light coating of sauce.

TIP: To get the best results, use a metal wok as it holds its heat better and gives the dish a more smoky taste, but if you are using a non-stick frying pan, make sure you cook over the highest heat (you want the pork to fry, not boil).

BABI CHIN

FRAGRANT PORK WITH SHIITAKE MUSHROOMS

Serves 4

8 large dried shiitake mushrooms

1 tbsp vegetable oil

4 small, round shallots (about 100g), peeled

6 garlic cloves, thinly sliced

1 tbsp ground coriander

4 star anise

600g pork belly, cut into 2.5cm cubes

1 tbsp dark soy sauce

1½ tbsp light soy sauce

1½ tsp caster sugar

¼ tsp salt

¼ tsp of ground white pepper

1 litre water

This is a Nyonya dish which I didn't try until I moved to the UK. I was flicking through a magazine and this dish caught my eye because of its name. *Chin* was my maiden name and *babi* means pig, so I guess it is quite apt as I am as greedy as a pig when it comes to food and life! This is a great dish to cook a day in advance, as the flavours develop with time.

Put the dried shiitake mushrooms in a bowl, cover with cold water and set aside to rehydrate for 2 hours. You can speed up the rehydration by covering them with just-boiled water, if you prefer.

Heat the oil in a frying pan, add the shallots and garlic, and fry for 2 minutes until fragrant. Add the coriander and star anise, cook for 1 minute, then add the cubed pork and fry for 2 minutes, stirring once or twice.

Drain and squeeze any excess water from the mushrooms, then remove the stalks. Add the mushrooms to the pork, then add both the soy sauces, sugar, salt and white pepper, along with the water and bring to the boil. Lower the heat, cover and simmer for 1¾ hours, until the pork is tender.

Remove from the heat and leave to cool, then transfer to a container and chill in the fridge overnight. A layer of fat will solidify on the top – you can simply scoop this away then reheat the pork to serve.

NUGGET DAGING BABI MERAH
RED PORK BELLY NUGGETS

Serves 4

500g rindless pork belly, cut into
    5cm-long strips, then 1.5cm-thick
    chunks
300ml vegetable oil, for deep-frying

For the marinade

2 x 4cm cubes of red fermented
    bean curd, crushed with a fork
    to form a paste
1 small egg
1 tsp caster sugar
½ tsp five-spice powder
1 garlic clove, crushed
½ tbsp oyster sauce
1 tbsp Shaoxing wine or dry sherry
½ tsp ground white pepper
½ tsp toasted sesame oil
4 tbsp tapioca flour or cornflour

I discovered these little beauties on a visit home to Ipoh. They were so tender and tasty, I vowed to recreate them at home.

Mix all the ingredients for the marinade in a bowl. Add the pork belly chunks and leave to marinate for at least 30 minutes, or longer (covered) in the fridge. If you're chilling the pork, let it come back to room temperature before you fry it.

Heat the vegetable oil in a wok or large frying pan. To test if the oil is hot enough, carefully drop a little piece of the belly in the oil and if it sizzles vigorously and floats to the top, the oil is ready. Deep-fry a small batch of the marinated pork belly over a medium heat for about 5 minutes, until golden and crispy. Remove with a metal slotted spoon and leave to drain on kitchen paper.

Make sure the oil is hot enough before you start cooking the next batch. Repeat until all the pork is cooked, then serve immediately.

TIP: If you are not eating the nuggets immediately, you can re-fry them in oil or place them in the oven at 180°C/160°C fan/ 350°F/Gas 4 for 4 minutes.

RUSUK MERAH
RED-BRAISED PORK RIBS

Serves 4

1kg pork ribs, cut into 5cm-long
   pieces (separating the bones) –
   your butcher can do this
1 tbsp vegetable oil
30g ginger, peeled and finely diced
2 garlic cloves, finely diced
1½ large cubes of red fermented
   bean curd or 2 small 4cm cubes,
   crushed with a fork to form a paste
4 tsp caster sugar
2 tbsp dark soy sauce
1 tbsp rice wine
500ml chicken stock (made with 1
   tbsp chicken stock powder –
   or home-made stock

For the marinade
2 tbsp rice wine
1 tbsp toasted sesame oil
1 tbsp light soy sauce
1 tbsp cornflour

I love ribs – who doesn't?! – but like most people I like my ribs a certain way. I particularly love those with gristle on that are so tender that the meat is clinging to the bone for dear life. They also need to be strong in flavour, juicy and a bit saucy. This recipe fulfills my requirements and I hope it does yours. We tend to eat them with rice but I have enjoyed them with fries too. You can also serve the ribs as a snack or starter with some tangy slaw.

Place the pork ribs in a large bowl and rub with the marinade ingredients. Set aside for 20 minutes.

Heat the oil in a wok or large saucepan until smoking, then add the marinated pork ribs and stir-fry until they turn light brown. Lower the heat to medium and add ginger and garlic. Stir-fry for 30 seconds, then add the mashed red bean curd and sugar and mix well.

Stir in the dark soy sauce and rice wine, then add the chicken stock and bring to the boil.

Turn down the heat, cover and simmer for 50 minutes. Check the ribs from time to time and give them a stir. If you don't have a lid for your wok or pan, make one with foil. After 50 minutes, uncover and simmer for a further 15 minutes, until the ribs are tender and the sauce is glossy.

AYAM GORENG MAMAK
TURMERIC 'MAMAK STYLE' FRIED CHICKEN

Makes 4 pieces

4 chicken thighs, skin on, excess fat
and skin trimmed off (retaining a
little for testing the oil
temperature)
300ml vegetable oil, for deep-frying

For the marinade
1 tbsp turmeric
¾ tsp chicken stock powder
¼ tsp salt
¼ tsp caster sugar
½ tsp chilli powder (optional)
4 tbsp coconut milk

I first had this chicken on a holiday to Pangkor Island with
Andrew. Now every time we make a trip to Pangkor we always
go to the shop and take away that yummy golden fried chicken.
Over the years I have tried to replicate it at home and this
captures it pretty well.

Place the thighs so they are sitting on the surface skin-side
down then, using a small knife, stab the chicken flesh a few
times to help the marinade penetrate the meat. Place the
chicken thighs in a bowl and rub with the marinade ingredients
then cover and chill for at least 4 hours or overnight. Let the
chicken come back to room temperature before you fry it.

Heat the oil in a wok or a saucepan over a medium heat.
Drop a bit of the trimmed chicken skin in the oil and if it sizzles
vigorously, the oil is ready.

Using a pair of tongs, gently lower the marinated chicken
thighs into the oil skin-side down and fry for 5–6 minutes.
Turn them over with tongs and fry for a further 5–8 minutes,
depending on their size. Using a ladle, gently pour the oil over
the skin continuously to ensure the skin is crispy.

Make sure they are cooked by lifting 1 out and cutting a slit
in the thickest part of the thigh to check for pinkness. If it isn't
cooked through, put it back into the oil and fry until cooked.

KARI AYAM
MALAYSIAN CHICKEN CURRY AND POTATOES

Serves 4

4 large chicken thighs, bone in and
    skin on
2 medium potatoes, peeled and cut
    into small chunks
1 tbsp vegetable oil
4 tbsp home-made Curry Paste
    (page 32), or shop-bought
    Malaysian chicken curry paste
300ml water
100ml coconut milk
handful of coriander, leaves torn
lime wedges, to serve

For the marinade

1 tbsp home-made Curry Paste
    (page 32) or shop-bought
    Malaysian chicken curry paste
1 tsp salt
1 tbsp coconut milk

This classic Malaysian curry is a fairly regular staple at home in Malaysia. You can make this wonderful curry using my home-made paste or you can buy Malaysian chicken curry paste. Serve with Roti Canai (page 68) or Turmeric Rice (page 96). A great vegetable accompaniment is Stir-fried Lettuce (page 190).

Place the chicken thighs in a bowl and add all the marinade ingredients. Mix together, then leave to marinate at room temperature for 20 minutes.

Meanwhile, cook the potatoes in a saucepan of boiling water for 10 minutes, until they are nearly cooked through. Drain and set aside.

Heat the oil in a wok or large frying pan, place the marinated chicken in the pan skin-side down and brown for about 3 minutes.

Add the curry paste, water and coconut milk and bring to the boil, then reduce the heat and simmer uncovered for 30 minutes. Add the potatoes then simmer for a further 5–8 minutes, until the sauce thickens and the potatoes are cooked through. Sprinkle with coriander and serve with lime wedges.

AYAM KAPITAN
CAPTAIN'S CHICKEN CURRY

Serves 4–6

1 tbsp turmeric
½ tbsp salt
½ tbsp cold water
4 chicken legs, separated into
    thighs and drumsticks
100ml vegetable oil, for deep-frying
250ml coconut milk
1 lemongrass stalk, bashed
2 fresh Kaffir lime leaves
1 tbsp chicken stock powder
1 tbsp caster sugar
3 tbsp tamarind concentrate
crispy shallots, to serve
plain rice or Roti Jala (page 128),
    to serve

For the spice paste
20 dried red Kashmiri chillies
20g of fresh root ginger, peeled and
    roughly chopped
20g galangal, peeled and roughly
    chopped
2 lemongrass stalks (tender base
    only), chopped
15 small, round shallots (about
    175g), peeled and chopped
3 candlenuts or macadamia nuts
2 garlic cloves
1 tbsp vegetable oil

This is a Nyonya dish (a fusion of Chinese and Malay cuisine). I love it for its depth of flavour, and the tamarind really cuts through the richness of the coconut milk, resulting in a dish that is light but leaves a gentle tingle on your lips.

Traditionally this dish contains belacan (shrimp paste), but I prefer it without.

Mix the turmeric, salt and water together then put the chicken pieces in a bowl and rub with the turmeric mixture. Cover and leave to marinate in the fridge overnight if you have time. Alternatively, set aside at room temperature for 30 minutes.

For the spice paste, bring some water to the boil in a small saucepan, add the dried chillies and boil for 5 minutes, then remove from the heat. Leave the chillies to sit in the hot water for at least 15 minutes to soften, then drain and split them lengthways. Remove the seeds with the blade of your knife and discard. Cut the deseeded chillies in half.

Put all the ingredients for the spice paste, including the deseeded rehydrated chillies, in the bowl of a food processor or a blender and blitz until smooth.

Heat the oil in a wok or heavy-based casserole dish. Fry the marinated chicken in batches for 5–8 minutes, until browned. Remove the chicken and set aside on kitchen paper.

Carefully pour out half of the oil into a heat-proof container and return the wok or pan to the heat. Fry the spice paste for about 10 minutes in the remaining oil, stirring often to avoid it sticking to the pan and burning (please don't be alarmed at the amount of oil – if you don't use enough oil, your paste will burn).

Add the fried chicken and stir to coat the pieces in the paste, then add the coconut milk, bashed lemongrass and Kaffir lime leaves. Cook for a further 5 minutes.

Add the chicken stock powder, sugar and tamarind concentrate then taste and adjust the seasoning if necessary. Cook uncovered for 25–30 minutes over a medium heat until the chicken is cooked through, stirring often to avoid burning.

Sprinkle with crispy shallots and serve with rice of Roti Jala.

AYAM LADA HITAM & GAJUS
STIR-FRIED BLACK PEPPER CHICKEN
WITH CASHEWS

Serves 2

2 skinless, boneless chicken thighs,
  cut into 1cm strips
2 tsp oyster sauce
60g raw or roasted cashews
1 tbsp vegetable oil
1½ tsp whole black peppercorns,
  coarsely ground in a pestle
  and mortar
1 garlic clove, finely chopped
½ tsp caster sugar
large pinch of salt
2 tbsp water

Andrew and I had been going out for a few weeks and everything was wonderful. I wanted to give a small party to celebrate and I invited some of our friends along. I asked everyone to bring a dish and, wanting to impress him, I said I was cooking a dish too. Andrew brought Duck a l'Orange and I brought this dish, only unbeknown to everyone, it had actually been cooked by my mum. Everyone raved about how amazing it was. Andrew found out much later and never let me live it down. I have since learned how to make it though, and every time I do, he remarks that I was a cheat! If you want to impress your other half, cook this! Serve with rice, or wrap in iceberg lettuce leaves.

Place the chicken strips in a bowl and coat them in 1 teaspoon of oyster sauce. Set aside to marinate for 20 minutes.

Preheat the oven to 180°C/160°C fan/350°F/Gas 4. Tip the raw cashews onto a roasting tray and roast for 10–15 minutes, shaking the tray occasionally, until golden brown. Remove and set aside to cool. Skip this step if you're using roasted cashews.

Heat the oil in a wok or large frying pan over a medium heat and add the ground peppercorns. Fry for 30 seconds, until the peppercorns are fragrant, then add the marinated chicken and garlic.

Turn up the heat and stir-fry the chicken for 2–3 minutes, until it turns opaque. Add the remaining oyster sauce, the sugar and salt. Incorporate well and add the roasted cashews. Stir-fry for a further 30 seconds, then add the water to deglaze the wok or pan. Make sure the chicken is cooked through and remove from the heat.

KARI KAMBING INDIA
INDIAN MUTTON CURRY

Serves 4

2 tbsp vegetable oil
4 cloves
4 cardamom pods, lightly crushed
1 cinnamon stick (about 5cm)
4 small, round shallots, thinly sliced
1 sprig of curry leaves, leaves
    stripped
1 star anise
15g of fresh root ginger, peeled and
    finely chopped
2 garlic cloves, finely chopped
750g mutton, cut into 5cm cubes
500ml water
1 tsp salt
1½ tsp tamarind concentrate
185ml coconut milk

For the curry paste

3 tbsp Malaysian curry powder
    or Madras curry powder
½ tsp fennel seeds, toasted
    and ground
3 tbsp water

Whenever I visit a Mamak stall, I have some mutton curry to go with my Roti Canai (page 68) or Nasi Kandar. Mamak stalls feature stainless steel chairs and tables, rows and rows of curries and fried dishes, and a very noisy crowd. You are always offered a choice of plain, pilau or biryani rice (I always choose plain rice). Then you simply point to whatever takes your fancy and carry the plate to your table. The idea of Nasi Kandar is that whatever curries you choose, the gravy from them will marry well together. And you wash it all down with ice-cold Teh Tarik (page 232). So now if you find yourself in Malaysia, go and try Nasi Kandar! Or try this curry, with Turmeric Rice (page 96).

The term mutton in Malaysia is often used to refer to goat meat but in the UK it tends to be sheep. The meat can be tougher, so it is perfect for slow cooking which makes it flavoursome and tender. If you cannot source mutton, lamb neck fillet is a good alternative, but reduce the cooking time to just over one hour.

Mix the ingredients for the curry paste together, then set aside.

Heat the oil in a wok or large frying pan, add the cloves, cardamom and cinnamon stick and fry for 1 minute, until fragrant. Add the shallots, curry leaves, star anise, ginger and garlic and fry, stirring, until the shallots have softened.

Add the mutton to the pan and fry for 5 minutes, until no longer pink. Add the water, salt and tamarind concentrate. Bring to the boil then lower the heat and simmer uncovered for 1½ hours, stirring it from time to time. If it gets too dry before the mutton is tender, add a little more water.

Add the coconut milk and continue to simmer for a further 30 minutes, or until the mutton is tender.

SAMBAL HATI AINON
CHICKEN LIVER CURRY

Serves 4–6

1 tsp turmeric
½ tsp salt
3 tsp water
400g chicken livers, trimmed
   of sinew
200ml vegetable oil
4 tomatoes, quartered
5 spring onions, cut into 5cm
   batons
3 tbsp water
1 tsp chicken stock powder

For the spice paste

15 dried red Kashmiri chillies
   (about 6g)
40g dried shrimps
250g small, round shallots, peeled
   and roughly chopped
1 tsp shrimp paste

When I first moved to London I lived with a lovely Malaysian lady called Ainon who was an incredible cook. Out of all her wonderful dishes, this is the one I loved most. Serve this with lots of plain white rice and eat with your fingers!

Mix the turmeric, salt and water together in a bowl. Place the livers in the bowl, stir, cover and leave to marinate in the fridge for 4 hours.

For the spice paste, bring some water to the boil in a small saucepan, add the dried chillies and boil for 5 minutes, then remove from the heat. Leave the chillies to sit in the hot water for at least 15 minutes to soften while you prepare the other ingredients for the spice paste.

Place the dried shrimps in a heat-proof bowl, cover with boiling water and leave to rehydrate for 5 minutes. Drain and set aside.

Put the shallots in a blender and blitz until smooth. Add the rehydrated shrimps.

Once the dried chillies have softened, drain and split them lengthways. Remove the seeds with the blade of your knife and discard. Cut the deseeded chillies in half. Add the chillies to the blender and blitz again, then add the shrimp paste and blend the paste until smooth.

Remove the livers from the fridge 5 minutes before you want to cook them. Heat the oil in a wok or large frying pan, add the chicken livers and fry for about 8 minutes, turning them so that they brown on both sides. Be careful, as the livers will spit when they hit the pan, due to the water content in the marinade. Use a splatter guard if you have one. Transfer the livers to a tray lined with kitchen paper. Discard about 130ml of the oil.

Fry the spice paste in the remaining oil for 10 minutes, stirring frequently. Add the tomatoes, fry for another 5 minutes until they start to soften, then mash them into the sauce.

Return the chicken livers to the pan with the spring onions and cook for 2–3 minutes, then add the water and chicken stock powder. Stir and cook for a further minute then remove from the heat.

DAGING LEMBU DAN SADERI
STIR-FRIED BEEF AND CELERY

Serves 2–4

250g rib-eye steak, cut into thin
strips
1 tsp Chinese fermented black
beans (optional)
4 celery sticks, trimmed
2 tbsp vegetable oil
1 tsp whole black peppercorns,
slightly crushed
2 garlic cloves, chopped
1 tbsp oyster sauce
2 tbsp water

For the marinade
1½ tsp cornflour
1 tsp light soy sauce
pinch of ground white pepper

The star of the dish here is the celery. It's an undervalued vegetable and often an afterthought thrown into salads, soup stock, served as crudités or with a Bloody Mary. But I love this vegetable. If I can have it stir-fried with loads of garlic, salt and white rice, I am a happy girl. I find the combination of medium-rare beef and celery divine, so here is my version of Cantonese black bean and beef, given a celery oomph. Serve it with plenty of rice or Congee (page 108).

Mix the ingredients for the marinade together in a bowl, add the beef and stir to coat, then set aside for 20 minutes.

Soak the black beans, if using, in a bowl of cold water for 5 minutes, then drain.

Using a vegetable peeler, carefully peel a thin layer off the celery sticks, to ensure they're not stringy. Then, cut them into 4 × 1cm batons.

Heat half the oil in wok or frying pan until smoking, then throw in the marinated beef and fry over a high heat for 30 seconds. Remove the beef and set aside. There might be bits of beef left in the wok or pan but don't worry, it all adds to the flavour of the dish.

Turn down the heat to medium, add the remaining oil and the crushed peppercorns, drained black beans and garlic and fry for 1 minute until fragrant (be careful not to burn the mixture).

Add the celery batons and fry for 2–3 minutes, then return the beef to the pan, add the oyster sauce and water. Stir and cook for a further 30 seconds. Serve immediately.

RAMLY BURGER SPECIAL
RAMLY-STYLE BURGER (THE ULTIMATE WHOPPER)

Makes 2 burgers

150g minced beef
100g minced pork (not lean)
large knob of butter

For the marinade

1 tsp onion granules
1 tsp garlic granules
1 tsp light soy sauce
1 tsp Malaysian curry powder or
    other curry powder
1 tsp cornflour
½ tsp salt
¼ tsp caster sugar
large pinch of ground white pepper

To serve

2 free-range eggs
2 slices of processed cheese (such
    as Dairylea)
4 tbsp mayonnaise
2 good quality burger buns, toasted
4 lettuce leaves (iceberg works best)
3 tbsp Maggi Chilli Sauce or sweet
    chilli sauce
1 tomato, sliced

Ramly Burger is a Malaysian company that specialises in meat patties. Not far from our house in Ipoh, there is a stall where nightclubbers head for a 'dirty' burger after a night of partying. Their famous 'Ramly burger special' is a beef patty wrapped in egg then smothered in mayo and Maggi Chilli Sauce. This is my take, but I wanted to make it even dirtier, so this is a whopper. It's not exactly diet-friendly but it's worth it!

Combine the marinade ingredients in a bowl, mix in the minced beef and pork, cover and leave to marinate in the fridge for at least 1 hour, or overnight.

When you're ready to make the burgers, let the marinated meat come to room temperature then divide it into 4 round balls and flatten them with the palm of your hand.

Heat the butter in a non-stick frying pan over a medium heat. Fry half of the patties for about 2 minutes on each side. If you prefer them well done, cook them for longer. Transfer the cooked patties to a tray lined with kitchen paper.

Pour some of the fat from the frying pan into a small heat-proof bowl and set aside, then return the pan to the heat. Lightly beat 1 egg and pour it into the pan, swirling the pan so the egg covers the base of the pan, like a pancake. When the egg starts to cook through, place a cooked patty on the egg and wrap the egg around it. Remove and set aside. Repeat with the other egg and a second patty.

Pour some of the reserved fat into the frying pan and fry the remaining patties for 2 minutes on each side. Place the cheese slices on top of each patty and continue to cook for 2 minutes. Turn off the heat and leave them in the pan while you assemble the burgers.

Spread a generous layer of mayonnaise onto 1 side of a toasted bun, top with a piece of lettuce, then the patty encased in egg, spread this patty with more mayonnaise and chilli sauce, followed by the patty covered with cheese. Top with the tomato slices and another piece of lettuce. Repeat with the other burger.

Tuck in, with plenty of napkins to hand!

FISH AND SEAFOOD

There is an abundance of fresh, affordable seafood and fish available in Malaysia. My hometown of Ipoh is only an hour and a half away from the coast, so we're spoilt for choice. I once travelled to the seaside town Lumut where I witnessed fishermen hauling in their fresh catch and sorting them before packing them in ice for sale at the wet markets. I've tried to get aboard one of those fishing boats, but tradition dictates that no women are allowed, for fear of bad luck! Well, I'll just stick to cooking the fish then.

Whenever I travel back to Malaysia I make a point of eating as much fish and seafood as I can, and each of these dishes brings me very happy memories.

IKAN KUKUS SOS TIRAM
DAN MINYAK BAWANG PUTIH

STEAMED HAKE WITH GARLIC OIL
AND OYSTER SAUCE

Serves 2

1 spring onion, finely sliced
   lengthways into strips
small handful of coriander leaves,
   torn
2 hake fillets (about 150g each),
   skin on
2 tbsp Garlic Oil (page 38)
2 tbsp oyster sauce

Steaming fish is my family's favourite way to cook it, as it remains moist and steaming locks in all the nutrients. When I first took Alexa back to Malaysia, my mum got an order of fresh fish for her in every day. She would simply steam the fish with a bit of garlic oil and oyster sauce. Alexa loves eating fish this way with some plain rice on the side. This recipe also works well with seabass and salmon. Bear in mind that the cooking time will vary with different fish.

Place a steamer ring at the bottom of a wok. Boil some water and pour it into the wok, up to the level of the ring. Place the wok over a medium heat and bring it to the boil, then lower the heat a little.

Place the spring onion strips in a bowl of ice-cold water with the coriander: this will keep them fresh while the fish steams.

Place the fillets of hake skin-side up in a shallow, heat-proof bowl, making sure they are not overlapping, then add the garlic oil and oyster sauce.

Transfer the bowl to the steamer ring, cover the wok and steam for 5 minutes. Uncover and add three-quarters of the spring onion and coriander leaves to the bowl. Re-cover and steam for a further 8 minutes. Carefully remove the bowl from the wok, sprinkle the rest of the spring onion and coriander leaves over the fish and serve immediately.

SEABASS GORENG KECAP MANIS
PAN-FRIED SEABASS WITH KECAP MANIS

Serves 2

1 tbsp cornflour
pinch of sea salt
2 seabass fillets, skin on
3 tbsp vegetable oil
1 tbsp sweet soy sauce
coriander leaves, torn, to garnish

Pan-frying is a great way to cook fish and I particularly love the flaky fish in this recipe. When I've nearly finished the fish and there are just little bits drenched in sweet soy sauce, I tip a generous amount of white rice onto them and mix the remaining fish, soy and rice together. My family know I love the flaky bits so they always leave theirs for me. This dish is also lovely served with Congee (page 108).

Place the cornflour on a plate or tray and sprinkle over the salt. Coat the fillets on both sides with a light covering of cornflour.

Heat the oil in a frying pan, gently shake the excess flour off the fish, then place the fillets skin-side down in the pan and fry for 2 minutes. Do not move the fish around the pan while it fries.

Flip the fillets gently and fry skin-side up for a further 1½ minutes (a little longer if the fillets are thick). Remove from the heat and let the fillets sit in the pan for another 30 seconds.

Transfer the fish to a plate, drizzle them with the soy sauce and pour three-quarters of the oil from the pan onto the fillets. It will sizzle.

Garnish with torn coriander.

IKAN BAKAR
ROAST SKATE WITH TANGY SAMBAL

Serves 2

2 tbsp vegetable oil
2 fresh Kaffir lime leaves,
    finely sliced
½ tsp chicken stock powder
¼ tsp light soy sauce
1½ tsp tamarind concentrate paste
½ tsp caster sugar
2 large pieces of banana leaf, cut
    into 56 × 27cm rectangles
1 skate wing (about 300g)
 lime wedges, to serve
pickled shallots (page 39),
    to serve (optional)

For the spice paste
3 dried red Kashmiri chillies
1 fresh red chilli
5 small, round shallots, peeled
    and chopped
1 garlic clove
1 tsp shrimp paste (belacan)
1 tsp vegetable oil

TIPS: Make sure the banana leaves
don't have any holes by holding
them up to the light. Boiling the
banana leaves make them more
pliable and easy to fold.

Use scissors to cut the fresh
Kaffir lime leaves.

Most street-food stalls in Malaysia sell an array of fish and cook it to order, and the skate is usually grilled in a banana leaf to protect its delicate flesh and retain all the flavour. Banana leaves can be found in Oriental supermarkets (though you can also use foil).

Put the dried chillies for the spice paste in a heat-proof bowl, cover with boiling water and set aside for 10 minutes.

Place all the ingredients for the spice paste, including the soaked chillies, in a blender and blitz until smooth.

Heat the 2 tablespoons of oil in a small frying pan over a medium heat and add the spice paste and Kaffir lime leaves. Fry for about 5 minutes, stirring, until fragrant. Add the chicken stock powder, soy sauce, tamarind paste and sugar, and fry for a further 2 minutes, stirring. Remove from the heat and leave to cool completely.

If you're using banana leaves, fill the wok three-quarters full with water. Bring to the boil. Loosely fold the leaves and cook them – 1 at a time – in the boiling water for 3 minutes to soften. Carefully push them down with a wooden spoon into the water to fully immerse them. Remove and shake off the excess water.

Place the skate wing in the middle of 1 of the soaked banana leaf pieces (or a large piece of foil), with the leaf lying lengthways on the work surface. Cut a few slits on the skate wing and cover both sides with the spice paste, pushing some of the mixture into the slits.

Enclose the foil around the wing to make a parcel, or – if you are using banana leaves – place the second piece on top of the fish lying it horizontally over the fish, perpendicular to the first piece of leaf, forming a 'T' shape. Fold the bottom up and the top down, then fold the right edge in followed by the left. Secure the package with string.

Preheat the oven to 200°C/180°C fan/400°F/Gas 6. Roast the parcel in the oven for 20–25 minutes. To check it's cooked, insert a probe thermometer into the fish, through the parcel wrapping – it should be a minimum of 62°C. Alternatively, cook the parcel on the barbecue for 25–30 minutes. Once cooked, squeeze over the lime and serve with the shallots, if using.

KETAM CILI DENGAN MANTOU GORENG
CHILLI CRAB WITH FRIED MANTOU

Serves 4

1 live medium brown crab (about
  1.1kg), chilled for at least 2 hours
500ml vegetable oil, for deep-frying
4 frozen steam buns
1 tsp fermented soya beans
  (optional)
1 fresh red chilli, chopped
2 garlic cloves, chopped
25g of fresh root ginger, peeled and
  finely julienned
½ onion, chopped

For the sauce
60ml tomato ketchup
60ml sweet chilli sauce
1 tbsp sweet soy sauce
100ml water
1 tsp caster sugar
¼ tsp salt
1 tsp tamarind concentrate

For the garnish
1 spring onion, cut into fine strips
handful of coriander leaves

My mum cooks crab very simply, by steaming it with nothing added. However, I love to serve crab with steam buns, which can be found in Oriental supermarkets.

Mix all the ingredients for the sauce together and set aside.

Place the chilled crab onto its back with its belly facing up. Grip the crab firmly (holding its body) and, using a sharp thin knife, plunge the blade firmly into the crab at the pointed tip of the triangle fold. This will kill the crab quickly. Leave for 10 minutes, with the knife in place, then remove the knife carefully.

Pry open the shell and the body. You need quite a bit of muscle for this. Put the shell aside and retain the brown meat inside. Remove the gills (known as 'dead mans finger's').

Cut the body into 4–6 pieces. Using the back of the knife or a pestle, gently crack the claws and the legs of the crab.

Leave the crab pieces to drain on kitchen paper.

Heat the oil in a wok until smoking, then deep-fry the crab pieces in batches for 4–5 minutes, until the shell has an orange tinge and the flesh is white throughout. Remove the crab carefully with a slotted spoon and drain it on fresh pieces of kitchen paper and set aside.

Using the same oil, over a medium heat, deep-fry the frozen buns for about 5 minutes, turning them over halfway through the cooking time, until they are golden brown all over and cooked through. Remove carefully with a slotted spoon and drain on kitchen paper. Transfer the buns to a low oven to keep warm.

Put a second wok over the heat if you have one. If you don't, carefully pour most of the oil from the wok into a heat-proof bowl and place it somewhere safe to cool, retaining 2 tablespoons in the wok for the next step.

Heat 2 tablespoons of the oil you used to deep-fry the crab and buns in the wok and add the soya beans, if using, chilli, garlic, ginger and onion. Stir-fry over a medium heat until fragrant and soft. Add the sauce and incorporate well. Increase the heat and bring to the boil. Add the crab pieces and cook for a further 5–8 minutes. Mix the crab well into the sauce.

Dish up and garnish with spring onion and coriander. Serve with the fried steam buns.

 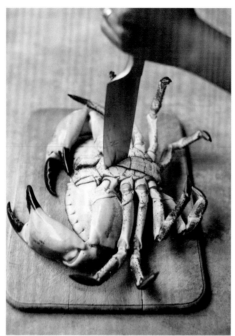 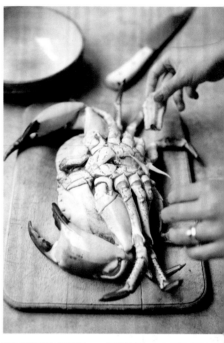

171

UDANG MENTEGA DAN BAWANG PUTIH
BUTTER GARLIC PRAWNS

Serves 2

300ml vegetable oil
6 large raw whole tiger prawns (shell
   and heads on)
15g butter
1 garlic clove, crushed
3 bird's eye chillies, finely sliced
15 fresh curry leaves
1 tsp light soy sauce
1 tsp caster sugar
3 raw egg yolks

Andrew and I shared our first butter garlic prawns on holiday in Malaysia, and every time we return we seek them out, as the dish brings back so many memories. Fresh curry leaves are a must, as they impart such a lovely fragrance, and give the dish a distinctive taste, which perfectly complements the butter. It really is finger lickin' good! Serve with plain steamed rice, if you like.

Heat the oil in a wok or frying pan until hot. Deep-fry the prawns for 1½ minutes, until they turn pink and crispy. Remove with a slotted spoon and set aside to drain on kitchen paper.

In another wok or frying pan, melt the butter then add the garlic, chillies and curry leaves and fry for about 1 minute over a medium–high heat, until fragrant. Add the soy sauce, sugar and fried prawns, and stir-fry for a further 30 seconds.

Place the egg yolks in a small fine-mesh sieve over the pan, and push them through with a teaspoon into the prawn mixture. This is to allow the eggs to trickle down slowly and remove any impurities. Fry, stirring continuously, until you've use up all the eggs. The egg should be crispy on the edges.

Remove from the heat and serve immediately.

SAMBAL UDANG MAK
MUM'S SAMBAL PRAWNS

Serves 4

240g green beans, trimmed and
cut in half diagonally
500g raw, peeled tiger prawns
6 tbsp vegetable oil
6 tbsp tamarind concentrate (you
can buy this in Oriental
supermarkets – it is ready to use),
alternatively use 8 tbsp lime juice
3 tsp chicken stock powder (or 1½
chicken stock cubes)
1½ tbsp caster sugar
2 tbsp water

For the spice paste

8 lemongrass stalks (tender base
only), roughly chopped
24 dried red Kashmiri chillies
20 small, round shallots, roughly
chopped
6 candlenuts or macadamia nuts
(optional)
½ tsp shrimp paste (belacan)
2 tbsp vegetable oil

Whenever my mum makes this dish, I polish it off with four or five bowls of rice. She makes it with Malaysian petai beans but I use standard green beans. Make loads of rice to go with this dish as you will need it. After my mum has dished out the prawns, she always tips a little bit of rice into the wok to mop up the sauce. Try to buy the best prawns you can find: the better the prawns, the better the dish.

Place all the ingredients for the spice paste in a blender and blitz until they form a smooth paste.

Blanch the green beans in lightly salted water for 3 minutes. Scoop out and rinse under cold running water. Using the same pot of water, blanch the prawns for 1 minute and as soon as they turn from grey to red, remove them from the pan and set aside.

Heat the oil in a wok or large frying pan over a medium heat. Add the paste and fry for 8–10 minutes, stirring, until fragrant. Add the tamarind, chicken stock powder and sugar and incorporate well. Taste and re-adjust the seasoning if necessary. Add the blanched prawns, green beans and water. Cook for 2–4 minutes, until the prawns and beans are cooked through (don't overcook the prawns as they will become rubbery). Serve immediately.

TIP: Tamarind can make prawns squidgy and unappealing in texture, but blanching them first ensures they stay firm and are affected less by the acidity of the tamarind. Prawns don't need much cooking, so the seasoning of the sauce has to be right before putting the prawns and beans in.

SOTONG TELUR MASIN
CRISPY SQUID IN SALTED EGG YOLKS

Serves 4

2 salted eggs
500ml vegetable oil, plus 2 tbsp oil
    for frying the egg yolks
350g fresh squid, cleaned and cut
    into 1.5cm rings
1 stalk of fresh curry leaves, leaves
    stripped

For the batter
45g tapioca flour
50g plain flour
1 tsp chicken stock powder
½ tsp caster sugar
30g butter, melted
½ tsp bicarbonate of soda
1 tsp baking powder
150ml cold water

I love salted eggs. I can eat them just boiled with Congee (page 108) or with Sambal Belacan (page 34) and white rice. When I first travelled back to Malaysia after moving here, my best friend Diana took me to a seafood restaurant where they served this dish. On my return I immediately set about recreating it – it really takes deep-fried squid to a new (and very delicious) level.

Mix all the ingredients for the batter together in a bowl and set it aside to rest for 20 minutes.

Bring a small saucepan of water to the boil, add the salted eggs and simmer for 15 minutes. Lift them out with a slotted spoon and leave to cool. Peel away the shells, cut the eggs open and extract the yolks. Discard the whites. Mash the egg yolks in a bowl with a fork and set aside.

Heat the vegetable oil in a wok or deep saucepan. To test if the oil is hot enough, carefully drop a little of the batter in the oil and if it sizzles vigorously and floats to the top, the oil is ready. Pat the squid dry with kitchen paper. Mix the squid into the batter and stir to make sure they are well coated. Line a baking tray with kitchen paper, ready for the fried squid.

Fry the squid in batches, dropping them into the oil gently and carefully, making sure they don't touch each other. Fry for 3–4 minutes, until they are crispy and golden. Be careful not to overcrowd the pan.

Remove with a slotted spoon and transfer them to the paper-lined tray.

Heat 2 tablespoons of oil in a wok, then add the mashed egg yolks and curry leaves. Fry the egg yolks for around a minute, until they are foamy. Working quickly, add the squid to the wok and toss well, making sure the egg mixture coats the squid Remove from the heat and serve immediately.

TIP: You can use frozen squid, but make sure they are thoroughly defrosted and pat them dry before coating them in the batter.

SOTONG MASAK HITAM
BLACK SQUID

Serves 4

2 tbsp vegetable oil
400g fresh squid, cleaned and cut
  into 1.5cm rings
8g squid ink
2 tbsp water
2 tsp tamarind concentrate
½ tsp salt
¼ tsp chicken stock powder
1 tsp caster sugar
¼ tsp light soy sauce
pinch of ground black pepper

For the spice paste
½ onion
2 fresh red chillies
1 bird's eye chilli
¼ tsp turmeric
1 tsp vegetable oil

For our first ever holiday as a couple, Andrew and I went to Pangkor Island and stayed in a cheap hut by the beach; we were blissfully happy. Across from our beach was the exclusive Pangkor Laut Resort. We were students then, so would never have been able to afford to stay there, but Andrew promised to take me one day. He fulfilled his promise on our fifth wedding anniversary and it was magical.

Several years later I returned to Pangkor Laut to write a travel piece, and took our daughter, Alexa. I was so excited to be taking her to an island that meant so much to us. We went fishing with the head chef and then to the local town to see how the fishermen worked. We bought fresh squid and the chef cooked me a speciality of his called *sotong masak hitam* which basically means 'squid cooked in ink'. It wasn't the prettiest plate of food, I must admit, but it was the sweetest, most tender and flavoursome squid I have ever tasted. Here is my version of it, which I like to serve with plain rice.

Place all the spice paste ingredients in the bowl of a food processor or in a blender and blitz until smooth.

Heat the oil in a wok, add the spice paste and fry over a medium heat for about 5 minutes, stirring (do not let it burn). Add the squid rings to the wok and fry for 30 seconds, then add the squid ink, water and remaining ingredients and cook for about 4 minutes, until the squid is tender.

VEGETABLES
AND EGGS

I rarely eat a meal without vegetables. When I first met Andrew, he hardly touched vegetables, claiming they were bland. I couldn't understand this until I moved to the UK and realised that vegetables here are so often overcooked: they lose all their vibrant colour and most of their nutrients, and are so mushy they have no texture. Vegetables should be cooked quickly to lock in their nutrients and preserve their crunch.

I've included a couple of quick egg dishes in this chapter, which you can whip up in no time. I always have eggs in the pantry, as they are so versatile and if all else fails, I boil a couple. You can never go hungry with eggs around.

SALAD TAUGEH IPOH
WARM SALAD OF BEAN SPROUTS
WITH PORK CRACKLING

Serves 8

For the pork crackling
200g pork skin
coarse sea salt

800g bean sprouts
½ tsp ground white pepper
1 tsp toasted sesame oil
3 tbsp oyster sauce
2 tsp pork fat, rendered from the
    pork crackling

My hometown of Ipoh is famous for the quality of its bean sprouts. They are particularly fat and juicy. Legend has it that Ipoh's water and fresh air are responsible for their superb quality. I often eat them with just soy sauce, vegetable oil and ground white pepper, but here I combine my love of all things pork to create an explosion of flavours and textures. It's the pork crackling that takes time in this dish but it's worth it and while you are at it you might as well make more than you need so you can enjoy some leftovers!

First make the pork crackling. Preheat the oven to 180°C/160°C fan/350°F/Gas 4. Pat the pork skin dry with kitchen paper. Take 2 baking trays with a slight lip. Lay the pork skin-skin side up on 1 tray, sprinkle liberally with salt, cover with baking parchment and lay the other baking tray on top. Cover the top tray with something heavy and heat-proof: you could use a casserole dish (as long as it fits onto the tray safely). Transfer the trays to the oven and cook for 40 minutes, then increase the heat to 200°C/ 180°C fan/400°F/Gas 6 and cook for a further 30 minutes. If the pork is not fully 'crackled', put it back in the oven and check it every 5–10 minutes. Once it's ready, remove the weight, the top tray and the baking parchment, drain and reserve the fat from the bottom tray and set the crackling aside.

When you're just about ready to serve, cook the bean sprouts in boiling water for 2–3 minutes, then drain.

Combine the white pepper, sesame oil, oyster sauce and 2 teaspoons of the pork fat in a large mixing bowl. Add the warm bean sprouts and mix well.

Crush some pork crackling and sprinkle it liberally on top of the bean sprouts and serve immediately.

CENDAWEN–CENDAWEN HALIA DAN SHAOXING
STIR-FRIED MEDLEY OF MUSHROOMS WITH GINGER AND SHAOXING WINE

Serves 4

1 tbsp cornflour

50ml water

1 tbsp vegetable oil

3 garlic cloves, finely chopped

10g of fresh root ginger, peeled and thinly sliced

130g chestnut mushrooms, cut into 0.5cm-thick slices

60g fresh king oyster mushrooms, cut lengthways into 0.5cm-thick slices

60g fresh shiitake mushrooms, stems removed and discarded

60g fresh golden needle mushrooms, roots removed and clumps broken apart

60g fresh enoki mushrooms, roots removed and clumps broken apart

1 tbsp oyster sauce

2 tbsp Shaoxing wine

Mushrooms are Alexa's favourite vegetable, so I wanted to create a mushroom extravaganza for her. If you are a fan of mushrooms then I can guarantee you will love this. Serve as an accompaniment to a meat or fish dish, or just on its own with rice or noodles.

Mix the cornflour in a bowl with 1 tablespoon of cold water and set aside.

Heat the oil in a wok until it's smoking, then add the garlic and ginger and stir-fry for 30 seconds.

Add the chestnut mushrooms and half of the water and fry for 1 minute, then add the king oyster mushrooms and fry for a further minute. Add the shiitake mushrooms and fry for 1 minute, followed by the golden needle and enoki mushrooms, oyster sauce, Shaoxing wine and the remaining water. Stir to combine, then add the cornflour mixture to the mushrooms, bring to the boil and simmer until the sauce thickens. Remove from the heat and serve immediately.

KANGKUNG BELACAN
STIR-FRIED MORNING GLORY WITH SHRIMP PASTE

Serves 2

1 tbsp vegetable oil
200g kangkung or Chinese water
    spinach or Morning Glory,
    washed, drained and cut into
    5cm lengths
30ml water
1 tsp tamarind concentrate paste
1 tsp light soy sauce
½ tsp chicken stock powder

For the spice paste

1 tsp dried shrimps, soaked in water
    for 5 minutes
2 small, round shallots, peeled and
    chopped
2 fresh red chillies (de-seeded if
    preferred)
1½ tsp shrimp paste (belacan)
1 garlic clove

Kangkung is also known as Morning Glory or Chinese water spinach. A semiaquatic plant, its hollow stems allow it to breathe in water. We have it in abundance in Malaysia and it's delicious stir-fried. One of my favourite ways to cook it is to fry it with chillies and belacan (shrimp paste). This goes beautifully with a bowl of plain rice.

Place the dried shrimps in a heat-proof bowl, cover with boiling water and leave to rehydrate for 5 minutes. Drain and set aside.

Place all the ingredients for the spice paste, including the rehydrated shrimps, in a small blender or a pestle and mortar and blend or grind until you have a smooth paste.

Heat the oil in a wok or frying pan over a medium heat and add the spice paste. Fry for 5 minutes, stirring, until fragrant, then add the kangkung and water, and fry for about 1 minute until the leaves begin to wilt.

Add the tamarind paste, soy sauce and chicken stock powder and fry for a further minute then serve immediately.

KUBIS MINYAK HEBI
STIR-FRIED SWEETHEART CABBAGE
WITH SHRIMP CHILLI OIL

Serves 4

1 tbsp vegetable oil
3 dried red Kashmiri chillies, halved
    widthways
pinch of salt
1 Sweetheart or pointed spring
    cabbage, leaves separated and
    tough core removed, and cut into
    4cm pieces
1 tbsp Shrimp Chilli Oil (page 43)
1½ tsp chicken stock powder
½ tsp caster sugar
½ tsp rice wine vinegar

My favourite restaurant of all time is a Chinese place in London called Hunan. Between 15 and 25 dishes arrive at the table in one sitting, and one of the most delicious of them is Szechuan fried cabbage. Stir-frying the cabbage means it stays crunchy, and adding the vinegar at the end completely elevates it.

Heat the oil in a wok or large frying pan over a high heat until just smoking, then add the dried chillies and salt. Fry for a few seconds, then add the cabbage to the wok. Continue to fry over a high heat for 1 minute, then add the shrimp chilli oil, chicken stock powder and sugar. Continue to fry for about 1 minute until the cabbage leaves wilt but still remain crunchy. Sprinkle over the vinegar and remove from the heat. Serve immediately.

SAYUR GORENG
STIR-FRIED LETTUCE

Serves 4–6

2 tbsp vegetable oil
3 garlic cloves, roughly chopped
1 large iceberg lettuce, leaves
    separated and roughly halved
    (discard any leaves with holes)
2 tbsp oyster sauce
100ml water
a large pinch of white pepper

This is a light, refreshing accompaniment to almost any dish. The trick is to fry over a high heat, cooking the lettuce until it just wilts so that it remains crunchy.

Heat the oil in a wok or frying pan and fry the garlic for 2 minutes until fragrant. Add the lettuce leaves and stir.
   Pour in the oyster sauce and water, stirring to ensure all of the lettuce leaves are coated. Add the white pepper and cook for 4-5 minutes, until the leaves start to wilt but retain a crunch. Discard any remaining water in the frying pan before serving.

CHOI SUM SOS TIRAM

BABY CHOI SUM IN OYSTER SAUCE AND GARLIC OIL

Serves 2

200g baby choi sum
1 tbsp Garlic Oil (page 38)
1 tsp oyster sauce

Blanching is the simplest way to cook vegetables, and they're cooked so quickly that they retain their colour and nutrients. If you can't find baby choi sum, use pak choi instead.

Bring a saucepan of water to the boil, add the choi sum, cover and cook for 2 minutes.

Drain, transfer to a bowl and toss with the garlic oil and oyster sauce.

TIP: Other vegetables that work well are iceberg lettuce, broccoli, kai lan and Little Gem lettuce.

TELUR PAPA

PAPA'S FRIED EGGS

Serves 4

1 tbsp vegetable oil
4 free-range eggs
2 spring onions, finely chopped
1 red chilli, chopped (de-seeded
   if you prefer)
10g ginger, peeled and finely diced
1½ tbsp sweet soy sauce

My father and brother love fried eggs, but as a child I hated them. Then, as I grew up, my taste buds matured and I started to enjoy them. I wanted to add a bit of sassiness to a simple fried egg, so over time this dish was born as a tribute to my father. These are lovely served with plain rice.

Heat the oil in a non-stick frying pan and fry the eggs sunny-side up until the edges are crispy but the yolks are still soft. Transfer to a plate as soon as they're cooked to your liking.

Using the same pan, fry the spring onions, chilli and ginger until soft. Sprinkle the mixture on top of the eggs, drizzle with the sweet soy sauce, and serve immediately.

TELUR FOO YUNG CHOI SUM
EGG FOO YUNG WITH CHOI SUM AND ONION

Serves 4

2 medium free-range eggs
½ tsp chicken stock powder
large pinch of caster sugar
large pinch of salt
1 tsp vegetable oil
1 red or white onion, cut into
    half-moon slices
2 stalks of choi sum, roughly
    chopped

Egg foo yung, essentially an egg omelette, is a classic Asian dish. You can add different fillings such as roast pork or prawns, but as I'm trying to encourage Alexa to eat vegetables, I have been adding different veg to ours. Choi sum is available in most supermarkets, and it adds a welcome crunch, nutrients and colour to this dish. It's a perfect accompaniment for Steamed Minced Pork Rice (page 101).

Beat the eggs lightly in a mixing bowl and add the chicken stock powder, sugar and salt.

Heat the oil in a non-stick frying pan over a medium heat and fry the onion until soft. Add the choi sum and fry until it begins to wilt.

Distribute the choi sum evenly in the pan and pour in the beaten eggs, covering the vegetable mixture. Swirl the pan so the eggs cover the vegetables evenly.

Using a spatula and, working quickly, stir the eggs once, then leave the mixture until the eggs are cooked through and the mixture has slightly crispy edges. Using the edge of the spatula, cut the omelette in half and turn it over. Repeat with the other half. Cook for a further minute, then serve immediately.

'ENGLISH' FOOD

'English' food in Malaysia is a catch-all term for anything that is vaguely western. My earliest memory of Mum's 'English' fare is a wok-cooked spaghetti with minced pork, and a sauce made from tomato ketchup. Sounds strange, but my brother and I loved it and I can still remember how it tasted. My uncle once brought her a jar of pasta sauce from Australia but we hated it, much preferring her version!

This chapter features some classic European dishes with a Malaysian twist. I dedicate this section to my mum, ever the creative cook, who tried incredibly hard to give us something different: I have always marveled at her determination to attempt dishes she had never even tasted before.

KEDGEREE

Serves 4

250g undyed smoked haddock
100g raw peeled tiger or king
  prawns
15g butter
1 small onion, diced
1 garlic clove, finely chopped
1 tsp home-made Curry Paste
  (page 32) or shop-bought
200g basmati rice, rinsed and
  drained
100g frozen peas
2 medium free-range eggs
salt, to taste
handful of coriander leaves,
  chopped
lemon wedges, to serve

For the poaching liquid
150ml full-fat milk
200ml water
1 tbsp home-made Curry Paste
  (page 32) or shop-bought

When I first moved to the UK, I struggled with breakfast. In Malaysia we have a variety of noodles, rice and curry dishes to choose from for our first meal of the day. When I first stayed with Andrew's parents, after enduring two days of cereal and toast, I crept down to the kitchen to stir-fry spaghetti with bacon for breakfast – spaghetti was the closest thing they had to noodles in their cupboard! His parents came down and were utterly baffled. Realising I was homesick for a Malaysian breakfast, Andrew cooked me kedgeree and I couldn't have been happier. My version uses home-made curry paste rather than curry powder.

Combine the poaching liquid ingredients in a frying pan. Place the haddock in the liquid and bring to the boil. Turn down the heat and simmer for 8 minutes. After 6 minutes of the cooking time have passed, add the prawns. Remove the haddock and prawns from the poaching liquid and set aside, then transfer the liquid to a heat-proof measuring jug and make it up to 400ml with water. Set aside.

Melt the butter in a saucepan then add the onion, garlic and curry paste. Fry until the onions have softened. Add the rice to the pan and stir to coat it. Add the poaching liquid and simmer over a low heat for about 5 minutes, until all the liquid has been absorbed. Do not stir. When bubbles start to appear on the surface of the rice, add the peas, stir and turn off the heat. Cover the pan and leave to sit for 30 minutes.

Meanwhile, cook the eggs in boiling water for 5 minutes. When cool enough to handle, peel off the shells, cut the eggs into quarters and set aside. Flake the haddock and discard all the skin and bones.

Remove the lid from the rice pan and use a fork to fluff up the rice. Place the pan over a low heat, add the flaked haddock and the prawns, and stir gently to mix the fish and prawns into the rice. Warm through for about 3 minutes, season with salt if necessary, remove from the heat and serve with the quartered eggs on top. Sprinkle with coriander and serve with lemon wedges for squeezing.

FISH DAN CHIPS MALAYSIA

MALAYSIAN FISH AND CHIPS

Serves 2

320g skinless hake fillets, cut into
   5cm cubes
pinch of sea salt
300ml vegetable oil, for deep-frying
1 stalk fresh curry leaves, leaves
   stripped

For the sweet potato chips

1 tsp salt
1 tbsp Malaysian curry powder
1½ tbsp vegetable oil
1 large sweet potato (350–400g),
   peeled and cut into 7–10cm long
   chunky chips

For the batter

45g tapioca flour
50g plain flour
1 tsp salt
30g butter, melted
½ tsp bicarbonate of soda
1 tsp baking powder
150ml cold water
1 tsp Malaysian curry powder

For the spiced tartare sauce

2 tbsp good-quality mayonnaise
2 tbsp crème fraîche
1 tbsp home-made Curry Paste
   (page 32) or shop-bought
½ quantity pickled shallots
   (page 39), or shop-bought,
   finely chopped

When I was invited by the British High Commission to the launch of the Food is GREAT campaign in Kuala Lumpur, they asked me to think of a way to promote British food with a Malaysian influence, so I instantly thought of fish and chips. Here I cover the fish in a light and crispy spiced coating and fry it with curry leaves, then serve it with sweet potatoes chips tossed in Malaysian curry powder to give them a spicy kick.

Preheat the oven to 190°C/170°C fan/375°F/Gas 5.

Start by making the sweet potato chips: combine the salt, curry powder and vegetable oil and toss with the chips, making sure they're well coated. Place the sweet potato chips on a roasting tray large enough so that they can sit in a single layer, without overlapping each other. Roast in the oven for 30 minutes, or until they are cooked and crisp on the edges.

Meanwhile, mix all the ingredients for the batter together in a bowl and set aside to rest for 20 minutes, and mix all the ingredients for the tartare sauce in a bowl and keep in the fridge until you're ready to serve.

Season the fish with a pinch of salt and set aside.

Heat the oil for deep-frying in a wok over a medium heat until smoking. To test if the oil is hot enough, carefully drop a little of the batter in the oil and if it sizzles vigorously and floats to the top, the oil is ready. Line a baking tray with kitchen paper, ready for the fried fish.

Pat the fish dry with kitchen paper, then dip the fish cubes in the batter to coat them all over. Gently and carefully drop them one by one into the hot oil. Add the curry leaves to the oil. Fry the fish for about 2 minutes (in batches if necessary), until golden and crispy, turning them so that they brown on all sides. Remove with a slotted spoon and transfer them to the paper-lined tray.

Serve the fried fish with the sweet potato chips and spiced tartare sauce, and a few of the fried curry leaves.

MACARONI BABI
PORK MACARONI

Serves 2

200g minced pork (not lean)
100g macaroni
2 tsp garlic oil (page 38)
750ml water
¾ tbsp chicken stock powder

For the marinade
large pinch of ground white pepper
1 tbsp light soy sauce
½ tsp caster sugar
1 tbsp cornflour

This macaroni is my ultimate comfort food, I love it for breakfast, or when I'm feeling under the weather. Everything in this recipe is super quick, including the broth, but if you have more time on your hands, my Simple Pork and Anchovy Broth (page 85) makes a delicious base.

Mix the minced pork in a bowl with the marinade ingredients and set aside to sit at room temperature for 10 minutes.

Cook the pasta in a large saucepan of boiling, salted water according to the packet instructions, but undercook it slightly, as it will finish cooking with the sauce. Drain, drizzle with half the garlic oil, and set aside.

Place the water and chicken stock powder in a saucepan and bring to the boil.

Using a teaspoon, scoop out a little of the marinated pork mixture into your hand and roughly shape it into a ball (about the size of a 50p coin). Drop the ball into the stock. Repeat until you've used up all the minced pork mixture.

Bring the stock to the boil again and add the pasta. Cook for 5 minutes.

Divide the pasta, pork balls and stock between 2 bowls and drizzle with the remaining garlic oil. Eat in your PJs (optional).

MUM'S STEAMED CHICKEN, BACON AND EGG JAW-DROPPER

Serves 2

1 tsp salt
1 chicken leg
thumb-sized piece of fresh root
   ginger, cut into 1cm-thick slices
5 slices of smoked streaky bacon
2 medium free-range eggs,
   hard-boiled and peeled
2 tbsp mayonnaise
pinch of ground white pepper
½ tsp English mustard
4 thick slices of white bread, to serve
sprinkle of crispy shallots (optional)

My friends were always envious of the food I brought to school every morning. I had two breakfasts, one early in the morning on the way to school and one at about 10am during break time. My mum made me this particular sandwich quite often, and I would always get hungry looks from my friends. Despite the delicious traditional food served in our brilliant canteen, the sight of something vaguely 'European' intrigued my classmates. Never one to do things by halves, my mum's 'jaw-dropper' was and continues to be a serious sandwich. Before long, she was making triple the amount for my best friends at school and twenty years on it's still renowned!

Rub the salt all over the chicken and set aside for 20 minutes at room temperature.

Place a steamer ring at the bottom of a wok. Boil some water and pour it into the wok, up to the level of the ring. Place the wok over a medium heat and bring to the boil, then turn down the heat.

Place the ginger in a shallow heat-proof bowl and the chicken leg on top of the ginger. Place the bowl on the steamer ring, cover the wok and steam for 30 minutes.

While the chicken is cooking, heat a non-stick frying pan and fry the bacon until the edges start to crisp up – you don't want the bacon to be completely crisp. Remove from the heat and cut the bacon into small pieces.

Remove the bowl from the wok and, when cool enough to handle, discard the ginger and tear the chicken meat into strips (discarding the skin and bones).

Combine the chicken strips, bacon pieces and hard-boiled eggs in a mixing bowl. Using a fork, slightly mash the eggs. Add the mayonnaise, pepper and English mustard. Mix well.

Serve between thick slices of white bread, adding the crispy shallots to the filling, if you like.

COP AYAM
MY CHILDHOOD CHICKEN 'CHOP'

Serves 2–4

2 de-boned chicken legs, skin on
(your butcher can de-bone them
for you)
90g Panko breadcrumbs
300ml vegetable oil, for deep-frying

For the marinade
½ tsp salt
1 medium free-range egg, lightly
beaten
dash of toasted sesame oil
large pinch of ground white pepper
1 tbsp cornflour

For the sauce
1 tbsp oyster sauce
1 tbsp Worcestershire sauce
½ tbsp light soy sauce
large pinch of ground white pepper
5 tbsp tomato ketchup
125ml water
3 tsp caster sugar
1 tsp vegetable oil
1 white onion, cut into half-moon
slices
1 garlic clove, chopped
2 medium tomatoes, chopped

'Chicken "chop"?', Andrew asked. 'Chicken doesn't have a "chop"', he said.

Well, I can't argue with that. Until I met Andrew, I honestly didn't know that chickens don't have 'chops' … Regardless, this is a very popular dish in Malaysia, often found at 'Western Food' stalls. Usually, the chicken legs are deep-fried and served with black pepper sauce or a tomato-based sauce. The accompaniments vary from stall-to-stall from rice to mixed vegetables or chips.

Place the de-boned chicken legs in a bowl, coat them in the marinade ingredients and set aside to marinate for at least 1 hour. If you're leaving them to marinate for longer than an hour, cover and transfer them to the fridge.

For the sauces, mix the oyster sauce, Worcestershire sauce, soy sauce, white pepper, tomato ketchup, water and sugar together in a bowl and set aside.

Heat the vegetable oil for the sauce in a frying pan, add the onion and garlic and fry until the onion begins to soften, then add the chopped tomatoes. Fry for a further 2 minutes, until the tomatoes have softened. Add the tomato ketchup mixture, stir and simmer for 3 minutes until thickened. Remove from the heat and set aside.

Place the breadcrumbs on a baking tray, add the marinated chicken legs and toss them in the breadcrumbs to coat them evenly.

Heat the vegetable oil for deep-frying in a wok over a medium heat. Drop a breadcrumb in it, and if it sizzles vigorously the oil is ready.

Carefully lower 1 chicken leg skin-side down into the oil. Using a metal ladle, pour hot oil continuously over the chicken and fry for 2 minutes on each side. Remove from the oil and leave to drain on kitchen paper while you fry the other leg.

Cut the fried chicken legs into thick slices and transfer them to plates.

Warm the sauce through and pour it generously over the chicken. Serve with plain rice or fried potatoes.

AYAM PANGGANG
ROAST CHICKEN

Serves 4–6

1 medium chicken (about 1.5kg)
1½ tbsp coarse sea salt
400ml can of full-fat coconut milk
(shake well before use)

For the spice paste
2 lemongrass stalks (tender base
only), roughly chopped
4 fresh green chillies, roughly sliced
(de-seed if preferred)
1 garlic clove, roughly chopped
1 tsp ground cumin
1 tsp ground coriander
1 tsp ground turmeric
½ tsp salt
vegetable oil, to loosen, if necessary

My favourite Sunday roast is a chicken. It always goes down well with the family and the leftovers can be used for stock, sandwiches or salads. I often infuse it with fresh and fragrant Malaysian flavours. Here, the coconut milk and spice paste make a wonderful 'gravy'. I serve it with Turmeric Rice (page 96) or plain rice and a large sprinkling of crispy shallots.

Place the chicken in a roasting tray, rub it all over with the salt and set aside.

Place all the ingredients for the spice paste in a blender and blitz until you have a smooth paste, adding a little oil to loosen the paste if it is too dry.

Rub the spice paste all over the chicken, then set aside to marinate at room temperature for 30 minutes. Preheat the oven to 180°C/160°C fan/350°F/Gas 4.

Place the chicken in the oven and cook for 1 hour, depending on its size, then pour the coconut milk over the chicken and cook for a further 20 minutes. To check if the chicken is cooked, insert a meat thermometer into the thickest part of the thigh. If it reads over 75°C the chicken is ready. If you don't have a meat thermometer, pierce the fattest part of the thigh with a skewer. The juices should run clear. If they don't, give the chicken a further 10 minutes in the oven.

Remove the chicken from the oven and let it rest for 30 minutes, covered with foil, then serve it with the coconut gravy.

SWEET THINGS

Malaysian desserts and sweet snacks are quite different to European ones and they can be a bit of an acquired taste, due to their unusual textures (which can be slightly gloopy). However, the most beautiful, delicious fruits are found in abundance throughout Asia and many form the basis of this chapter. I have included my favourite Malaysian desserts, as well as some we are more familiar with here in the UK, giving them a Malaysian twist. You can mix and match some of the sweets in here to create a more substantial dessert.

MESS MALAYSIA
MALAYSIAN MESS

Serves 4

For the coconut meringues
4 medium free-range egg whites
100g caster sugar
100g icing sugar, sifted
70g unsweetened desiccated
    coconut

For the compote
1 large ripe pineapple, peeled, cored
    and cut into 1cm cubes
2 star anise
½ lemongrass stalk, bashed
juice of 1 lime
70g soft dark brown sugar

For the whipped coconut cream
80ml coconut milk, chilled
200ml double cream, chilled

For the garnish
6 tbsp unsweetened desiccated
    coconut

I love Eton Mess and how the sweetness and crispiness of the meringue perfectly balances the tartness of the strawberries and is then mellowed by the cream. This recipe is a mix of these two delicious features, which I hope convey a sense that summer is just around the corner.

Start by making the meringue: whisk the egg whites in a spotlessly clean bowl until they form soft peaks, then whisk in half of the caster sugar, adding the rest gradually while continuously whisking, until the mixture is thick and glossy. Fold in the icing sugar and desiccated coconut.

Preheat the oven to 110°C/90°C fan/230°F/Gas ¼. Line 2 baking trays with baking parchment, securing them with little dots of meringue mixture at each corner, to keep the paper attached to the tray. Spoon about 12 dollops of meringue, roughly the size of tennis balls, onto the trays with a metal spoon.

Transfer the trays to the oven and bake the meringues for 1½ hours.

Put the cubed pineapple, star anise, bashed lemongrass and lime juice and sugar in a saucepan and bring to the boil. Reduce the heat and simmer uncovered for 25 minutes, until the pineapple is soft but still holds its shape. Remove from the heat and set aside. Discard the lemongrass and star anise.

Toast the desiccated coconut for the garnish in a dry frying pan for 5–7 minutes, until golden brown. Tip into a bowl and set aside to cool.

Using a hand-held electric whisk or stand mixer, whisk the coconut milk with the double cream until it forms soft peaks (it should still run off the spoon).

Assemble the dessert in bowls or small glass tumblers: start with a layer of pineapple, then broken bits of meringue, then coconut cream. Repeat the layers. Sprinkle with toasted desiccated coconut to serve.

PANDAN DAN KELAPA PANNA COTTA
PANDAN AND COCONUT PANNA COTTA
WITH MANGO AND PINEAPPLE

Serves 4

3 fresh pandan leaves, knotted
500ml coconut milk
500ml single cream
80g caster sugar
1 tsp vanilla bean paste
40g desiccated coconut
4 sheets of platinum grade leaf
    gelatine
½ ripe mango, peeled, stoned
    and diced
¼ small ripe pineapple, peeled
    and diced

Panna cotta is a classic Italian dessert, and I've infused it with classic Malaysian fruit flavours. I serve it in kilner jars but you can of course use bowls or dariole moulds. I don't like turning out panna cotta as it can be messy and I want to minimise the risk of it sliding off the plate! Adding the cream and coconut milk in stages makes the panna cotta lighter and fresher.

Put the pandan leaves, half the coconut milk, half the single cream, the sugar, vanilla paste and desiccated coconut in a saucepan and bring to just below boiling point. Remove the pan from the heat and leave to infuse for 30 minutes.

Place the gelatine leaves in a bowl of cold water and set aside for 5 minutes to soften.

Place the coconut and cream mixture back on the hob and heat through until warm. Squeeze the gelatine to get rid of excess water then stir it into the warm mixture until it has dissolved.

Strain the mixture through a fine sieve into a bowl, pressing the leaves with a wooden spoon to extract all the flavour and liquid.

Stir in the remaining cream and coconut milk and mix well. Divide the mixture between 4 × 500ml kilner jars or bowls. Cover and chill in the fridge for at least 4 hours to set.

Serve topped with diced mango and pineapple.

TIP: You can also serve this with Lychee and Kaffir Lime Granita (page 218) or Coconut Shortbread (page 214).

SHORTBREAD KELAPA
COCONUT SHORTBREAD

Makes about 40 shortbreads

45g unsweetened desiccated
    coconut
170g unsalted butter, at room
    temperature
100g caster sugar
½ tsp vanilla extract
½ tsp coconut extract
½ tsp coarse sea salt
170g plain flour, sifted

I was introduced to shortbread when I first moved to the UK, and on sinking my teeth into the crumbly little discs of buttery goodness, I was instantly obsessed. Shortbread adds crunch and texture to a dessert, and this one works brilliantly with my smooth and creamy Pandan and Coconut Panna Cotta (page 213). You can cut as many discs from the chilled dough as you like (just baking a few shortbread at a time, if you prefer), and the dough will keep for up to five days.

Scatter the desiccated coconut on a baking tray and roast in a hot oven or toast in a dry frying pan for 5–8 minutes, until golden brown. Remove and set aside to cool.

Beat the butter and sugar with a hand-held electric whisk or in a stand mixer until light and fluffy. Add the vanilla and coconut extracts and the salt.

Gradually add the flour to the butter and sugar, continuing to beat until all the flour has been added. Stir in the toasted coconut.

Place a piece of cling film on a flat surface. Divide the shortbread dough in half. Place 1 half on the cling film and shape it to form a 'sausage' about 4cm in diameter along the width of the cling film. Roll the bottom of the piece of cling film up over the dough, and roll it up, keeping the dough as smooth and round as possible, then twist both ends of the film so that it looks like a giant sweet. Repeat with the other half of the dough.

Place the dough 'sausages' in the fridge for at least 1 hour to firm up. Preheat the oven to 160°C/140°C fan/325°F/Gas 3 and line a baking tray with greaseproof paper.

To bake, remove the dough from the fridge, unwrap and cut the dough into 1cm-thick discs. Place on the lined baking tray, leaving about a 2.5cm gap between them as they will spread out while cooking.

Bake for 20 minutes, until golden brown, then remove from the oven and leave to cool.

KAYA
CARAMEL COCONUT CURD

Makes about 270ml

4 medium free-range egg yolks
150g caster sugar, plus 50g to make
  the caramel
3 fresh pandan leaves, cut into 5cm
  pieces
200ml coconut milk

Kaya (coconut curd) is very popular in Malaysia. There are two types – caramel and pandan – and both have a different flavour and colour (the pandan version is a very striking jade). My favourite way to eat *kaya* is probably the most common one: served sandwiched between two slices of toasted bread (traditionally toasted over charcoal) and a generous quantity of hard salted butter. The sweetness and creaminess of the *kaya* paired with the saltiness of the butter on smoky toasted white bread is heaven! This recipe requires an Asian version of a bain-marie, where a saucepan is placed inside a frying pan and is 'double boiled' so that the curd isn't cooked over a direct heat allowing it to cook more slowly, resulting in a smooth and creamy curd.

Place the egg yolks, caster sugar, pandan leaves and coconut milk in a stainless steel saucepan.

Place the saucepan in a wok or a deep-sided frying pan and fill the wok or frying pan with hot water (not too much though – the saucepan needs to stay flat on the wok, and too much water will make the saucepan float). Place this over a medium heat.

Stir the egg yolk mixture continuously with a rubber spatula for about 20 minutes, until the mixture thickens.

Place the sugar for the caramel in a separate small stainless steel saucepan, making sure it's evenly distributed over the surface, then melt and cook over a low heat for 4–5 minutes without stirring, until it turns a rich brown caramel colour, but be careful not to burn it.

Pour the caramel into the coconut mixture and stir to incorporate it. Cook for another 5–10 minutes, stirring frequently.

Strain the mixture through a fine sieve into a jug or pan, then pour it into a sterilised jam jar or kilner jar. Cover and leave to cool, then store in the fridge until ready to use. It will keep for up to 3–4 weeks in the fridge.

Spread on toast with a generous quantity of salted butter.

MENTEGA KACANG DAN KAYA FRENCH TOAST
PEANUT BUTTER AND KAYA FRENCH TOAST

Makes 2 slices of French toast

3 tbsp Caramel Coconut Curd
  (page 215)
4 thick slices of white bread
3 tbsp crunchy peanut butter
1 large free-range egg, lightly
  beaten
2 tbsp full-fat milk
knob of butter
golden syrup, to serve (optional)

This version of French toast is a hugely popular *kopitiams* (coffee shop) staple. The eggy bread is deep-fried, topped with salted butter and slathered with syrup. Clearly it's not diet-friendly, but it is delicious! I've pan-fried it so it becomes a marginally healthier (though still indulgent) breakfast dish or dessert. It's even more tasty served with crispy bacon, Kopitiam eggs (page 59) or fresh fruit.

Spread half of the curd on a slice of bread and half the peanut butter on another. Sandwich them together and set aside. Repeat with the other 2 slices of bread.

Place the beaten egg and milk in a shallow dish and beat together with a fork.

Dip the sandwiches into the egg mixture 1 at a time, making sure they are fully coated, leaving them to sit in the mixture for 30 seconds.

Melt the butter in a large frying pan over a medium heat and place the soaked sandwiches in the pan (or fry them 1 at a time if your pan isn't big enough). Cook until 1 side is brown all over and starting to crisp up, then flip over and cook the other side.

Remove from the heat, transfer to plates and drizzle with golden syrup, if you like.

TIP: If you don't fancy making your own Caramel Coconut Curd, buy it at the Oriental supermarket. It comes in jars and is available in two flavours: caramel or pandan.

LAICI DAN KAFFIR GRANITA
LYCHEE AND KAFFIR LIME GRANITA

Serves 4–6

567g can of lychees
8 fresh Kaffir lime leaves, torn
50g caster sugar
juice of 3 limes and grated zest of 1

Whenever I'm coming up with a dessert idea, I think about flavours as well as textures. I cater for private dinner parties, and I love it as I get to design the menu according to my client's preference, the occasion and their story. I designed this granita to give a burst of freshness to a dessert. I've adored lychees since I was a child and the citrusy flavour of Kaffir reminds me of my mum's Kaffir plant.

I like to serve this granita on its own, or with Pandan and Coconut Panna Cotta (page 213).

Empty the can of lychees and syrup into the bowl of a blender or food processor. Blitz until smooth, then pour the liquid into a saucepan along with the lime juice and zest.

Scrunch up the torn Kaffir lime leaves and add them to the lychees. Add the sugar and place the pan over a medium heat. Bring the pan to the boil then turn off the heat and let the Kaffir lime leaves infuse the lychee liquid for at least 1 hour.

Strain the liquid through a fine sieve into a shallow container, cover and transfer to the freezer. Check the granita every hour for 4–6 hours, scraping the ice crystals from the outside edge to the middle with a fork, breaking them up until it reaches a snow-like consistency.

HUP TOH SOH
MUM'S CHINESE NEW YEAR COOKIES

Makes about 80 cookies

250g cashews
600g plain flour, sifted
2 tsp baking powder
⅓ tsp bicarbonate of soda
2 tsp salt
250g icing sugar, plus extra
    for dusting
375ml vegetable oil
2 large free-range egg yolks, beaten

These cookies hold such fond memories for me. Every year when I was a child my mum and I would make these cookies. Well, she would make and I would watch! Then she would box them up to send to her clients a month before Chinese New Year. My mum loves to make cookies or other edible treats to send as gifts, and I think handmade treats are special as they are always made with love, time, and effort and with the best ingredients available. These are crumbly and smell fantastic, and are also very easy to make. You may wish to reduce the quantities here if you aren't making them as gifts.

Preheat the oven to 180°C/160°C fan/350°F/Gas 4. Tip the cashews onto a roasting tray and roast for 10 minutes until lightly golden. Remove and leave to cool, then roughly chop. Turn the oven down to 160°C/140°C fan/325°F/Gas 3.

Place all the ingredients except the egg yolks in a large mixing bowl and mix well. The dough will feel a little crumbly, but this is normal and it will come together when it's rolled out.

Take a small batch of dough, place it on a flat work surface dusted with icing sugar and roll it out until it is about 1cm thick. Cut out cookies with your favourite cookie cutter.

Place on a baking tray, leaving space between each cookie. Brush with egg yolk and bake for 20–25 minutes until golden brown. Remove and leave to cool on a wire rack. They will keep for up to 5 days in an airtight container.

BUBUR PULUT HITAM
BLACK RICE PUDDING

Serves 4–6

100g black glutinous rice
50g plain pudding rice
1 litre water
2 fresh pandan leaves, knotted
120g caster sugar
250ml full-fat coconut milk, plus
    extra for drizzling
¼ tsp salt
ripe mango, peeled, stoned and
    sliced (optional)

Very occasionally at night, when we couldn't sleep and my mum's sweet tooth beckoned, we would drive to Rainbow City food court, named after the nightclub opposite, where a dessert stall sold this pudding. My dad would have the almond milk pudding, my mum the black rice pudding and my brother and I the peanut pudding. This is my mum's favourite.

Rinse both types of rice in several changes of cold water, then leave to soak overnight.

The next day, drain the rice and place it in a large saucepan. Add the water and pandan leaves and bring to the boil. Lower the heat and simmer for about 1 hour. Check from time to time, especially towards the end of the cooking time, to make sure the rice doesn't stick to the bottom of the pan. The rice is ready when it is soft, creamy and porridge-like, but still has a slight bite. If it looks too dry, add a little water.

Add the sugar to the rice and taste for sweetness, adding more if you want it sweeter, then cook for a further 10 minutes and remove from heat.

In a separate saucepan, heat the coconut milk gently with the salt. Once it reaches boiling point, remove from the heat.

Transfer to heat-proof serving bowls and drizzle with a couple of spoonfuls of coconut milk .

Serve it warm on its own or with sliced fresh sweet mangoes. It's equally delicious served cold.

KUIH KETAYAP
MALAYSIAN COCONUT-FILLED PANCAKES

Serves 4–6

For the pandan juice
6–8 fresh pandan leaves, cut into
    small chunks
150ml water

For the sweet coconut filling
125g palm sugar, roughly chopped
225ml cold water
1 fresh pandan leaf, knotted
100g freshly grated coconut or
    unsweetened desiccated coconut

For the pancakes
150g plain flour
¼ tsp salt
2 small free-range eggs, beaten
100ml pandan juice (see above)
150ml coconut milk
65ml water

1 tbsp vegetable oil, plus extra
    for frying

TIP: You can make the filling and juice up to 3 hours in advance (the pancake batter will keep in the fridge overnight).

This is one of my favourite traditional Malaysian desserts. These are lovely in the morning or after dinner, and make a great alternative to the more typical lemon and sugar combination.

To make the pandan juice, put the leaves and water in a blender or the bowl of a food processor and blend until smooth. Strain the liquid through a fine sieve or through muslin into a bowl to extract the juice. Discard the leaves.

To make the coconut filling, dissolve the sugar with the water in a saucepan over a medium heat and simmer for 5 minutes. Add the knotted pandan leaf and grated or desiccated coconut (you might need to add a little more water to the pan if using desiccated coconut, to help it soften). Cook over a low heat for about 15 minutes, until almost all the water has evaporated. The mixture should be sweet and glossy. Remove the pan from the heat and set aside to cool.

To make the pancake batter, sift the flour and salt into a mixing bowl. Make a well in the centre and add the eggs, the pandan juice and coconut milk. Whisk the dry ingredients gradually into the wet to make a smooth batter.

Thin the batter with the water and stir in the oil. Cover the bowl and set aside to rest for 20–30 minutes.

Heat 1 tablespoon of oil in a small frying pan, then drain the excess oil from the pan once it's hot. Ladle some of the pancake batter into the pan and swirl the pan around until you have an even, thin layer. When the batter sets and the pancake starts to brown at the edges, flip it and cook the other side for a further 10–15 seconds.

Move the pancake to a plate and place a piece of greaseproof paper on top to avoid the next pancake sticking to the first one. Repeat with another ladleful of batter, making more pancakes until all the batter is used up.

If the mixture gets too thick, thin it out with more water or coconut milk.

To fill a pancake, put a spoonful of the coconut mixture just above the bottom edge of a pancake, fold the pancake over the filling, fold in the sides to enclose the filling, and roll it up.

SWEET THINGS

AISKRIM GOLD BLEND POPO DALAM ROTI GORENG

POPO'S GOLD BLEND ICE CREAM IN DEEP-FRIED BUNS

Makes about 1 litre (serves 4)

3 tbsp Nescafé Gold Blend instant coffee
1½ tbsp hot water
300ml double cream
175g condensed milk
½ tsp vanilla bean paste
2 tbsp Tia Maria
300ml vegetable oil
4 frozen milk buns

In keeping with the Chinese tradition of a mother living with her son, my popo (grandmother) lived with us, as my father was her only son. Her daily breakfast routine involved porridge cooked in condensed milk and a cup of Gold Blend Nescafé coffee, sweetened with condensed milk with a soft-boiled egg dropped in it. It sounds strange, but the flavours really do work. As a child, I found this combination fascinating and I'd always beg her to let me have some of this peculiar, comforting concoction. I've never let go of this food memory and decided to take elements of my popo's breakfast to create an ice cream, and combine it with one of my favourite sweet snacks, the milk bun.

Mix the coffee with the hot water to form a paste, making sure the granules are completely dissolved. Set aside.

Place the double cream, coffee, condensed milk, vanilla bean paste and Tia Maria in the bowl of a stand mixer fitted with the balloon whisk attachment, and whisk on medium–high speed until the mixture forms soft peaks (be careful not to overwhip). Alternatively, use a hand-held electric whisk.

Transfer the mixture to a loaf tin, cover with cling film and place in the freezer for 4–6 hours.

When you're ready to serve, heat the oil in a wok over a medium heat, drop the buns in and fry them evenly all over for 4–5 minutes until golden brown. You can fry them from frozen, but take time to fry them gently and not on too high a heat: you want them to cook through but not burn on the outside. Drain on kitchen paper and leave to cool a little.

Slice each bun horizontally through the middle. Scoop a generous ball of coffee ice cream onto one half and top with the other half bun.

Devour and go on a diet another day.

TIP: You can serve the ice cream with a brioche bun instead of a milk bun, if you like.

POPIAH PISANG
BANANA SPRING ROLLS

Makes 4 spring rolls

4 x 8.5cm spring roll sheets
4 tbsp caster sugar, plus extra
   for dusting
4 whole, just-ripe bananas, peeled
2 tbsp ground cinnamon
300ml vegetable oil

Deep-fried bananas are a popular sweet snack in Malaysia. They're usually found at roadside food stalls, where there is a constant batch on the go. Although I grew up eating fried bananas, I find they can be a bit greasy and overly sweet, so these spring rolls are a lovely crispy alternative. They're delicious on their own but better still with a scoop of peanut butter ice cream or drizzled with chocolate sauce.

Place 1 of the spring roll sheets on a flat work surface in front of you, to form a diamond shape. Sprinkle some caster sugar across the sheet horizontally 4cm up from the bottom of the sheet.

Place a whole banana on top of the sugar, then roll the triangle up tightly, tucking in the sides as you go and brushing the edges with water. Transfer the spring roll to a plate and put in the fridge for 30 minutes to firm up. Repeat with the remaining spring roll sheets and bananas.

Mix the cinnamon and sugar in a bowl. Place the bowl on a flat tray.

Heat the oil in a wok or a wide saucepan until it reaches 180°C on a probe thermometer. Alternatively, drop a tiny bit of spring roll sheet into the oil to test if the oil is hot enough: the piece of sheet should sizzle vigorously and quickly float to the top. Carefully slide in the spring rolls. Deep-fry for 2–3 minutes on each side, until the rolls are golden brown and crispy all over. Remove and drain briefly on kitchen paper. Place the spring rolls on the tray with the sugar and cinnamon and toss to coat generously.

FA SUNG TONG

PEANUT 'CANDY' WITH COCO POPS AND SESAME SEEDS

Serves 4–6

170g caster sugar
100g salted peanuts
25g Coco Pops
1 tbsp sesame seeds

This super-sweet candy is similar to peanut brittle and is made in much the same way. On a recent trip home to Malaysia, I had the best ever peanut candy, which was studded with puffed rice. I have used Coco Pops instead, as I love the combination of peanuts and chocolate. Warning: it is very moreish!

Line a baking tray with greaseproof paper.

Place the sugar in a stainless steel saucepan and melt it over a very low heat, until you have a rich, dark brown caramel. It will take up to 15 minutes to reach this stage. As the sugar cooks, use a wooden spatula to move the sugar from the edge of the pan into the middle so that the sugar melts evenly. Watch it carefully as it will burn very easily.

As soon as the sugar is ready (148–154°C on a sugar thermometer), add the peanuts, Coco Pops and sesame seeds. Mix well and quickly, then pour onto the lined tray and spread as thinly as possible. Leave to cool.

Once cool, break the peanut 'candy' into smaller pieces and store in an airtight container.

DRINKS

We have a wide variety of fresh fruit available in Malaysia, so it's easy to find refreshing drinks, made to order at street stalls. As a consequence, I find supermarket squash and cordials a little dull – I like my soft drinks and cocktails to be interesting and packed full of flavour.

A lot of these drinks can be made from ingredients you have left over from cooking other recipes in this book, such as pandan, chillies and lemongrass – waste-not want-not. Chin Chin!

TEH PANDAN
PANDAN TEA

Serves 2–4

4 fresh pandan leaves, roughly cut
  into 1cm pieces
1½ tbsp caster sugar
2 tsp gunpowder tea leaves
500ml water

I saw pandan tea on a menu in a Thai restaurant once, and was genuinely excited. It was served hot, and was very tasty, but I was disappointed to discover that it had been made from a packet, especially when it's so easy to make fresh. Here I've used leftover pandan leaves and infused them with gunpowder tea leaves. I like to serve it in Chinese tea cups.

Put the pandan leaves, sugar and tea leaves in a teapot.
    Bring the water to the boil and pour it into the teapot. Leave to infuse for 10 minutes, and serve hot, strained into cups.

TEH TARIK
PULLED TEA

Serves 4

500ml water
3 English Breakfast teabags
3 tbsp condensed milk

Teh tarik, a classic drink sweetened with condensed milk, is found at a lot of Mamak stalls. After the tea is mixed to the perfect level of sweetness, it is repeatedly poured from one jug to another to create a frothy top. The art of pouring is taken so seriously in Malaysia that they have tea-pulling competitions. For health and safety reasons I'd advise leaving that to the professionals! To create a frothy top I use a hand blender.
    It's best to serve pulled tea either very hot or very cold. Iced pulled tea is most refreshing – just add an extra tablespoon of condensed milk and let the tea cool before pouring it into a glass filled with plenty of ice.

Place the water in a small saucepan and bring to the boil. Drop the teabags into the pan, remove from the heat, and leave to infuse for about 3 minutes. Press the teabags in the water with a teaspoon to make a strong brew.
    Mix the condensed milk into the tea and, using a hand blender, blend the tea until you have a frothy top.
    Serve very hot or very cold.

JUS NENAS
FRESH PINEAPPLE JUICE

Serves 4

1 large pineapple, skin and needles
    removed, flesh cut into chunks
250ml cold water
juice of 1 lime
2 tbsp caster sugar
ice cubes, to serve

You can find decent cartons of pineapple juice here in the UK, but nothing beats the fresh kind.

If you have a juicer, juice the pineapple chunks in batches. Alternatively, place the pineapple chunks in the bowl of a food processor or blender and blend to a pulp. Strain the juice through a fine-mesh sieve into a mixing bowl and add the water. Using a spatula, stir the mixture in the sieve so you are left with pulp in the sieve and the juice underneath.

Mix the lime juice and sugar together and add them to the pineapple juice. Blitz the juice with a hand blender until the mixture is frothy and the sugar and lime juice are well incorporated.

Pour into glasses over plenty of ice, close your eyes and think of somewhere hot.

ICED LEMONGRASS TEA

Serves 4 (fills 4 high-ball glasses)

1 litre water
1 tbsp gunpowder tea leaves
4 lemongrass stalks, cut in half
    widthways and bashed
2½ tbsp caster sugar
ice cubes, to serve

Lemongrass is my favourite herb of all time. I just adore its flavour as well as its versatility. It's very refreshing on a hot day, especially when served alongside spicy food.

Bring the water to the boil in a saucepan then turn the heat down to low. Place the tea leaves and lemongrass pieces in the saucepan. Add the sugar and stir to dissolve.

Turn off the heat and leave to infuse for 30 minutes–1 hour. Once it's completely cool, drain through a fine-mesh sieve and pour into glasses filled with plenty of ice.

TIP: You can re-use the tea leaves and lemongrass stalks for another batch of tea. Leave to infuse a little longer (about 1 hour) to extract the flavour, as it will be less potent than the first batch.

WAIN ROSE, LIMAU, KAFFIR MOJITO
ROSE, LIME, MINT AND KAFFIR LIME MOJITO

Serves 2

8 fresh Kaffir lime leaves
8 fresh mint leaves
1 lime, cut into 6 wedges
ice cubes, to serve
200ml rosé wine
lemonade, for topping up (I like
    Schweppes or San Pellegrino
    Limonata)

A couple of years ago, we had a wonderful holiday in Polignano a Mare, a beautiful town in southern Italy. We went out for a pre-dinner drink one evening and the waiter brought me a rosé wine topped with soda made with local lemons. When I got back home, I tried replicating it with leftover Kaffir lime leaves and lemonade, and this reviving summer drink was born.

Divide the Kaffir lime and mint leaves and the lime wedges between 2 tall glasses, and crush them together. Leave for 5 minutes to infuse.
   Half-fill the glasses with ice, then add 100ml of wine to each glass and top up with lemonade.

TIP: If it is too sweet, add more lime. Some limes are juicier than others.

SERAI DAN KAFFIR GIN DAN TONIC
LEMONGRASS AND KAFFIR LIME GIN AND TONIC

Makes about 750ml

10 fresh Kaffir lime leaves
750ml bottle of gin
10 lemongrass tops or 5 whole
    lemongrass stalks, cut in half
    widthways and bashed
lime wedges, fresh Kaffir lime
    leaves (optional) and tonic water,
    to serve
ice cubes, to serve

I always have loads of lemongrass tops left over after making curry pastes, and this is a fantastic way of using them up. You can also keep Kaffir lime leaves in the freezer.

Scrunch up the kaffir lime leaves to encourage them to release their flavours.
   Pour yourself 50ml of gin and make a G&T! This makes room in the bottle for the aromatics.
   Place the bruised Kaffir leaves and lemongrass into the bottle of gin, replace the lid and leave to infuse for 24 hours.
   You can strain the liquid and decant it into another clean bottle if you wish – the gin will keep well in the freezer – but it never lasts that long in my house so I don't bother.
   Serve the gin with a squeeze of lime, 2 fresh Kaffir lime leaves (optional), tonic water and loads of ice in a large tumbler.

WHISKY AND GREEN TEA

Serves 2

1 cup of standard green tea
2 tsp caster sugar
50ml whisky
ice cubes, to serve

When I'm home in Malaysia I love a night on the tiles. The Malay drinking culture is different to that of the UK, with most drinks in bars bought by the bottle rather than by the glass, and rather than beer and wine, spirits are the norm. The most popular drink is whisky, which goes down a treat with sweetened green tea. This drink has fuelled many a night out with old friends …

Make a cup of green tea and add the sugar. Stir to dissolve then leave to cool.
　　Put 25ml of whisky in 2 short tumblers, fill to the top with ice and top up with sweetened green tea.

CHILLI DARK AND STORMY

Serves 2

50ml rum
1 bird's eye chilli, roughly sliced
1 lime, cut into 4 wedges
fiery ginger beer
ice cubes, to serve

Since having my daughter Alexa, we often have friends over to dinner, as it's easier than going out. I discovered this drink one summer when I was preparing dinner and accidently dropped some chillies into my rum. I couldn't be bothered to fish them out, and it was a pleasant surprise when I took a sip! I made a batch for our friends that night, which they loved. It will leave a tingle on your lips, so alter the amount of chillies depending on your tolerance of heat.

Place 25ml of rum in 2 short tumblers, add 2 slices of chilli and leave to infuse for about 10 minutes.
　　Squeeze 2 wedges of lime into each tumbler, leaving the wedges in the glass, then top up with ice and add ginger beer. Give it a good mix and serve very cold.

PANTRY AND EQUIPMENT INDEX

RECICPE INDEX

ACKNOWLEDGEMENTS

Writing a cookbook is seriously hard work! Despite this, I feel so proud and humbled to call myself an author, it has been a labour of love. I never imagined I'd one day bring out my own book, sharing a cuisine that's so important to me. It sounds clichéd but I couldn't have done it without the love and support of so many people and I would like to take this opportunity to thank them.

First and foremost, thank you to my incredibly supportive husband, Andrew. His unconditional love and unwavering faith have helped me find who I'm truly meant to be. He is my pillar of strength and the best babysitter in the world! My daughter, Alexa, encourages me to be a better cook every day. When she is fussy with her food, she teaches me perseverance and patience!

Thanks to my mother, who is the most amazing cook in the world (I'm biased, I know). She taught me to show love through food. I wish everyone could try her cooking. She is my greatest critic and the one that I still strive to impress!

I'm grateful to Nicola Pye, my beautiful friend who sent me the application form to MasterChef all those years ago, and who continues to offer love and encouragement.

Thank you to my wonderful agent, Louise Lamont at LBA, who has worked tirelessly to guide me through the world of publishing and who led me to Orion. I'm so appreciative of her dedication, honesty and belief in me.

Big thanks to Amanda Harris at Orion whose enthusiasm and vision for my book instantly won me over. Thanks also to Tamsin English, my editor, who is full of smiles and warm hugs, and who had her work cut out for her editing my lengthy first draft. I'm grateful to Laura Nickoll, my copy-editor, who took time to fine-tune my recipes so that they made sense to everyone else! Thank you to Clare Skeats and Lucie Stericker for the beautiful, striking design of the book.

To Mark McGinlay, Alice Morley and the sales, marketing and publicity teams at Orion: thank you. Here's hoping we can make #ping4hugh a reality!

This book would not have come alive without the help of some incredibly creative people. Orion put together a dream team including Laura Edwards, photographer extraordinaire: thank you for making my food look so effortlessly appealing. Thanks to Frankie Unsworth, a dynamo in the kitchen and one of the most talented cooks I have ever worked with. To Tamara Vos who tirelessly made all of the pastes for the shoot and who entertained us with her singing. To Olivia Wardle for being so precise and creative in the choosing of props: thank you for understanding the recipes and me, and for always selecting just the right thing to complement the food.

To my local butcher at Larkhall who consistently delivers incredible service and produce, and for always having the candy box ready for Alexa to keep her from running out of the shop!

To all my friends, family and social media followers: thank you for your enthusiasm for my recipes, your ongoing support and encouraging words. Every 'like' and 'follow' is like a hug and seal of approval that I'm doing something right. I hope you will love this book as much as I've loved writing it.

Thanks to my MasterChef family for allowing me to be part of it. Without you, I wouldn't be where I am today.

Finally, thank you to my former employer who made me redundant, sending me down a path so awesome I couldn't have contemplated in a million years!

First published in Great Britain in 2016
by Orion Publishing Group
Carmelite House, 50 Victoria Embankment
London EC4Y 0DZ
An Hachette UK Company

10 9 8 7 6 5 4 3 2 1

A CIP catalogue record for this book is available from the British Library.

ISBN: 978 1 4746 0149 8

Food photography: Laura Edwards
Page 42: Harry Trow
Page 140 © Shutterstock
Designer: Clare Skeats
Props stylist: Olivia Wardle
Food styling: Ping Coombes and Frankie Unsworth
Food styling assistant: Tamara Vos
Editor: Tamsin English
Copy-editor: Laura Nickoll

Printed and bound in China

The Orion Publishing Group's policy is to use papers that are natural, renewable and recyclable products and made from wood grown in sustainable forests. The logging and manufacturing processes are expected to conform to the environmental regulations of the country of origin.

www.orionbooks.co.uk

by
BOOK
or by
COOK
COOKING
EATING
SHARING

For more delicious recipes, features, videos and exclusives from Orion's cookery writers, and to sign up for our 'Recipe of the Week' email visit **bybookorbycook.co.uk**